SMALL CITY HOUSES

PETITES MAISONS DE VILLE

KLEINE STADTHÄUSER

SMALL CITY HOUSES
PETITES MAISONS DE VILLE
KLEINE STADTHÄUSER

EVERGREEN

EVERGREEN is an imprint of

Taschen GmbH

© 2006 TASCHEN GmbH

Hohenzollernring 53, D-50672 Köln

www.taschen.com

Editor Editrice Redakteur:
Simone Schleifer

English translation Traduction anglaise Englische Übersetzung:
Jane Wintle

French translation Traduction française Französische Übersetzung:
Marion Westerhoff

German translation Traduction allemande Deutsche Übersetzung:
Susanne Engler

Proof reading Relecture Korrektur lesen:
Matthew Clarke, Marie-Pierre Santamarina, Martin Rolshoven

Art director Direction artistique Art Direktor:
Mireia Casanovas Soley

Graphic design and layout Mise en page et maquette Graphische Gestaltung und Layout:
Diego González, Elisabet Rodríguez

Printed by Imprimé par Gedruckt durch:
Gráficas Toledo, Spain

ISBN: 3-8228-5143-4

The modern lifestyle and the changes that have occurred in society since the nineteenth century have led people to live in increasingly smaller spaces. Since then, the urban environment has become more and more the favored habitat for humans. The city exerts an inexplicable attraction on the masses and on modern technology, creating an interaction between the two in everyday life. This population boom in the cities, combined, in many cases, with the inability to expand further, has led to a shortage of floor space, resulting in an increase in housing prices. This situation obliges both people living alone-such as young people in their first home- and families to opt for small houses.

Innovative solutions to limited spaces are implemented in many different ways and reflect this contemporary lifestyle full of creativity and originality. When it comes to living comfortably in a small house, there are many practical resources available: for example, in new buildings or conversions, it is possible to eliminate rooms that are not essential, such as hallways and corridors, and add the saved space to the main living area.

Custom-designed furniture is another good option, as it always conforms to the taste of the occupants. Similarly, a single space is often assigned various uses, enabling a sitting room, for example, to also serve as a studio and bedroom. A design that takes advantage of simple lines, interplays of light or a color scheme all offer different ways of changing the appearance of rooms: thus, pale colors heighten the sensation of expansiveness and luminosity, while a few splashes of bright color can imbue a space with personality. Furthermore, some architectural and decorative styles, such as minimalism, are inherently favorable to the creation of simple, open spaces.

This book offers a selection of original, imaginative projects, representing the current urban living space. Apart from the variety of styles and programmatic requirements, all of them have something in common: the reduction to what is truly necessary from a house, generated through a limited amount of square feet.

Unique projects, created by worldwide famous designers, have been selected to reflect the new ways of inhabiting and experimenting with distribution, materials, textures and light. These projects are examples of interior micro-urbanism, of how design can mold a space to make it personal, functional and aesthetically pleasing.

Le style de vie moderne et l'évolution de la société depuis le dix-neuvième siècle ont contraint la population à vivre dans des espaces de plus en plus réduits. Dès lors et de plus en plus, l'environnement urbain devient l'habitat de prédilection. La ville exerce une attraction inexplicable sur les masses de population et la technologie moderne, entraînant une interaction de l'une sur l'autre au quotidien. Cet essor démographique des villes, très souvent lié à l'impossibilité de s'étendre davantage, conduit à une pénurie de surface habitable débouchant sur une augmentation du coût du logement. Situation obligeant à la fois les célibataires -les jeunes en quête du premier logis- et les familles à opter pour des petites maisons.

Les solutions innovantes pour pallier l'espace limité, et leurs multiples applications, reflètent ce style de vie contemporain empreint de créativité et d'originalité. En effet, une petite maison dispose aujourd'hui de toute une gamme de possibilités pour offrir un vrai confort de vie. A titre d'exemple, dans certaines habitations ou réhabilitations récentes, les pièces qui ne sont pas indispensables, à l'instar de halls d'entrée et de couloirs, sont supprimées pour gagner de la surface et amplifier l'espace de vie principal. Citons d'autres bonnes alternatives : un mobilier sur mesure offrant l'avantage d'être conforme aux goûts des occupants ou encore un espace unique multifonctionnel, à l'instar d'un séjour servant de studio ou de chambre à coucher. Un design tirant parti de la simplicité des lignes, des jeux de lumière ou combinaisons de couleurs sont autant de moyens de modifier l'apparence des pièces : les couleurs pâles amplifieront la luminosité et l'espace, tandis que quelques taches de couleurs vives le personnaliseront. A cela s'ajoutent certains styles architecturaux et de décoration d'intérieur qui, à l'instar du minimalisme, favorisent la création d'espaces simples et ouverts.

Cet ouvrage offre une sélection de projets originaux et imaginatifs, représentatifs de l'espace de vie urbain, quotidien. Outre la variété de styles et les exigences de programmes, tous ont le même dénominateur commun : la réduction d'une maison au strict minimum nécessaire due à la limitation des mètres carrés.

Des projets uniques, oeuvres de designers de réputation internationale, ont été sélectionnés pour refléter les nouvelles formes d'habitat et de concepts sur les plans de distribution, matériaux, textures et lumière. Ces projets sont des exemples de micro urbanisme intérieur, de l'art du design à façonner l'espace pour créer un univers personnel, fonctionnel et esthétique.

Der moderne Lebensstil und die Veränderungen, die in der Gesellschaft seit dem neunzehnten Jahrhundert stattfanden, haben dazu geführt, dass die Menschen in immer kleineren Wohnungen leben müssen. Die Stadt ist zum bevorzugten Wohnort der Menschen geworden. Sie fühlen sich auf unerklärliche Weise von den Massen, der modernen Technologie und der täglichen Interaktion dieser beiden Faktoren angezogen. Die Bevölkerungsexplosion in den Städten, die in vielen Fällen mit der Unmöglichkeit einer Erweiterung der Stadtfläche einhergeht, hat zu einer Bodenknappheit und damit zur Erhöhung der Immobilienpreise geführt. Diese Situation zwingt sowohl junge Leute, die ihre erste Wohnung beziehen, als auch Familien dazu, sich für ein kleines Haus zu entscheiden.

Innovative Lösungen für kleine Flächen werden auf viele verschiedene Weisen eingeführt und sie spiegeln den modernen Lebensstil voller Kreativität und Originalität wider. Wenn man mit allem notwendigen Komfort in einem kleinen Haus leben will, gibt es viele Mittel, die einem dabei helfen. So kann man zum Beispiel in Neubauten oder bei Umbauten Räume wegfallen lassen, die nicht unbedingt notwendig sind, wie Flure und Korridore, und den dadurch eingesparten Platz dem Wohnzimmer hinzufügen.

Eine andere Möglichkeit sind maßgefertigte Möbel, die dem Geschmack der Eigentümer entsprechen. Auch kann ein einziger Raum für verschiedene Zwecke benutzt werden, zum Beispiel ein Wohnzimmer kann auch als Studio oder Schlafzimmer dienen. Bei der Gestaltung muss man auf einfache Linien und auf das Spiel mit dem Licht und den Farben achten, weil dadurch das Erscheinungsbild eines Raumes geprägt wird. Blasse Farben verstärken den Eindruck von Weite und Helligkeit, während ein paar helle Farbtupfer einem Raum Charakter verleihen. Desweiteren gibt es Stilrichtungen in der Architektur und der Dekoration wie zum Beispiel den Minimalismus, die dazu beitragen, einfache und offene Räume zu schaffen.

In diesem Buch finden Sie eine Auswahl an originellen und einfallsreichen Bauprojekten, die die moderne Wohnweise in der Stadt zeigen. Obwohl verschiedene Stile und Haustypen gezeigt werden, ist ihnen allen etwas gemeinsam, nämlich die Beschränkung auf das, was wirklich in einem Haus notwendig ist, eine Beschränkung, die auf den begrenzten Raum zurückzuführen ist.

Es wurden einzigartige Häuser von berühmten Architekten und Innenarchitekten ausgewählt, um zu zeigen, wie man mit der Raumaufteilung, den Materialien, den Texturen und dem Licht experimentieren kann, um eine komfortable Wohnumgebung zu schaffen. Es handelt sich um Beispiele für einen inneren Mikrourbanismus, und dafür, wie man durch die Gestaltung einen Raum persönlich, funktionell und sehr ästhetisch machen kann.

SMALL CITY HOUSES
PETITES MAISONS DE VILLE
KLEINE STADTHÄUSER

Plastic House
Maison de plastique
Kunststoffhaus

Kengo Kuma & Associates

As concrete is both easy to ease and highly resistant, it has become the universal construction element par excellence – so much so that it has nearly replaced indigenous construction traditions. In this project, a house built for a prestigious photographer and his family, the architect established a new relationship with the environment by using a different material: FRP (fibreglass reinforced polyurethane). This is a plastic material 4 mm thick, injected in various shapes and sizes, with fibers that can make it resemble paper or bamboo. The exterior walls, terraces, staircases and floorboards are all made of FRP, which transforms the house into a box that irradiates a soft, filtered light. The habitability of the plastic house is derived from the physical characteristics of its surfaces and not from its distribution, as the material connects with our bodies through every detail.

Grâce à sa facilité d'emploi et à sa grande résistance, le béton est devenu l'élément de construction universel par excellence. En effet, il s'est pratiquement substitué aux traditions de construction autochtones. Dans ce projet de construction pour un prestigieux photographe et sa famille, l'architecte a créé une nouvelle relation avec l'environnement en employant un matériau différent : PRFV (polyuréthanne renforcé de fibres de verre). Il s'agit d'une matière plastique d'une épaisseur de 4 mm injectée sous diverses formes et formats, et qui grâce à ses propriétés de fibres, revêt parfois l'apparence de papier ou de bambou. L'ensemble des murs extérieurs, les terrasses, les escaliers et les plaques du sol sont en PRFV qui transforme la maison en une boîte de verre irradiant une douce luminosité tamisée. L'habitabilité de la maison de plastique découle de l'aspect matériel de ses surfaces et non de sa distribution, puisque la matière est en relation avec nos corps par le biais de chacun des détails.

Aufgrund der einfachen Anwendung und großen Festigkeit wurde Beton zu dem universellsten Baumaterial. Ein Beweis dafür ist, dass er praktisch alle einheimischen Bauformen ersetzt hat. Dieses Haus, das für einen bekannten Fotografen und seine Familie errichtet wurde, schafft eine neue Beziehung zur Umwelt durch die Benutzung eines anderen Materials: PU (glasfaserverstärktes Polyurethan). Es handelt sich um einen 4 mm dicken, gespritzten Kunststoff in verschiedenen Formen und Größen, der aufgrund der Eigenschaften seiner Fasern manchmal wie Papier und manchmal wie Bambus aussieht. Die gesamten Außenmauern, die Terrassen, die Treppen und die Bodenplatten bestehen aus glasfaserverstärktem PU, so dass das Haus zu einem Lichtkasten wird, der ein sanftes gefiltertes Licht ausstrahlt. Die Bewohnbarkeit dieses Kunststoffhauses beruht auf dem Aussehen der Oberflächenmaterialien und nicht auf der Aufteilung, weil dieses Material in jedem Detail mit unserem Körper in Kommunikation steht.

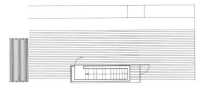

Second floor Deuxième étage Zweite Obergeschoss

First floor Premier étage Erstes Obergeschoss

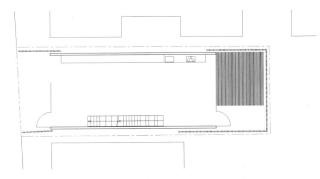

Ground floor Rez-de-chaussée Erdgeschoss

Basement Sous-sol Kellergeschoss

The exterior walls are made of FRP, which transforms the house into a box that irradiates a soft, filtered light.

Les murs extérieurs sont en PRFV, ce qui transforme la maison en une boîte de lumière irradiant une douce luminosité tamisée.

Die Außenmauern bestehen aus glasfaserverstärktem Polyurethan, so dass das Haus zu einem Lichtkasten wird, der ein zartes, gefiltertes Licht ausstrahlt.

The ground floor is a wide open space, used as kitchen, dining room, and living room and, if required, a photography studio.

Le rez-de-chaussée est un vaste espace ouvert, utilisé comme cuisine, salle à manger et salle de séjour, et au gré des besoins, comme studio de photos.

Das Erdgeschoss ist ein weiter, offener Raum, der als Küche, Speisezimmer und Wohnzimmer benutzt wird, und falls dies notwendig ist, auch als Fotostudio.

The steps of the staircase have been designed with special care in order to preserve the distinctive qualities of the material.

Les marches de l'escalier sont conçues avec un soin tout particulier pour conserver la singularité du matériau.

Die Stufen der Treppe wurden mit besonderer Sorgfalt gestaltet, um die Einzigartigkeit des Materials zu zeigen.

House in Saitama
Maison à Saitama
Haus in Saitama

Milligram Studio

This house, located in one of the busiest parts of the Japanese city of Saitama, was a challenge for the Milligram Studio team. The architects set the entire house in the middle of the street, propping the building a few meters above the ground. To do this they installed robust piles that hold up the metal base on which the house was constructed. They were able to give the cube-shape structure a feeling of weightlessness because of the lightness of the pillars. Pedestrians can easily circulate through the open space underneath. The first floor receives abundant sunlight, thanks to the terrace enclosed by a metal mesh that runs along the front of the house. The top floor is less open to the exterior, so white walls and appropriate furniture were chosen to enhance the feeling of light and spaciousness.

Cette habitation située dans une des zones les plus courues de la ville japonaise de Saitama s'est transformée en défi pour l'équipe du Milligram Studio. Les architectes ont renversé complètement l'habitation au milieu de la rue au moment d'élever sa structure quelques mètres au-dessus du niveau du terrain grâce à des supports résistants qui soutiennent une base métallique sur laquelle l'habitation est érigée. La structure en forme d'un volume cubique unique, parvient à transmettre une certaine sensation d'apesanteur grâce à la légèreté des piliers. En dessous, les passants peuvent circuler en toute liberté entre les espaces libres. Le premier étage reçoit la lumière du soleil, puisqu'il est pourvu d'une terrasse en mailles métalliques orientée à l'extérieur le long de la partie frontale de l'habitation. Au niveau supérieur, moins ouvert sur l'extérieur, le mobilier et le blanc des murs rehaussent la sensation d'espace.

Dieses Haus befindet sich in einem der geschäftigsten Viertel der japanischen Stadt Saitama. Für das Team vom Milligram Studio war dieses Projekt eine Herausforderung. Die Architekten errichteten das Haus in der Mitte der Straße, indem sie die Struktur einige Meter über dem Boden aufbauten. Dazu schufen sie widerstandsfähige Träger, die eine Grundstruktur aus Metall halten, über der sich das Haus erhebt. Das Gebäude besteht aus einer einzigen Würfelform, die aufgrund der Leichtigkeit der Säulen den Eindruck von Schwerelosigkeit entstehen lässt. Die Fußgänger können unbehindert den darunter entstandenen freien Raum durchschreiten. Durch eine Terrasse am vorderen Teil des Hauses, die aus einem Metallnetz besteht, fällt das Tageslicht in die erste Etage. Auf der oberen Etage, die nicht so offen nach außen ist, lassen die Möbel und die weißen Wände den Raum weiter wirken.

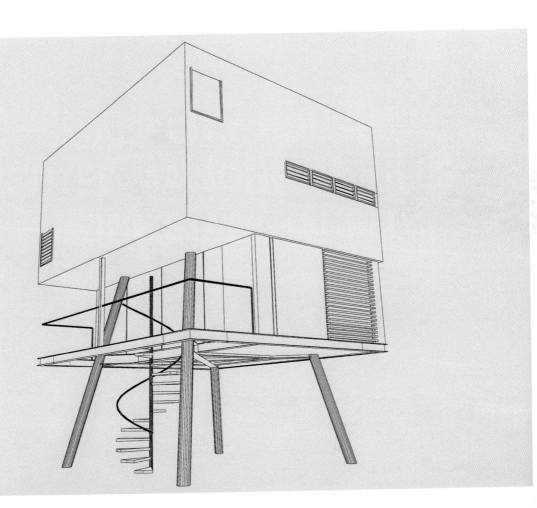

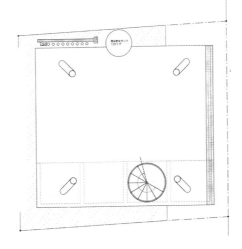

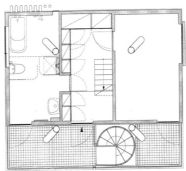

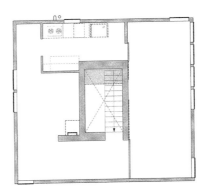

Plans Plans Grundrisse

The architects installed robust piles to hold up the metal base on which the house was constructed.

Les architectes ont utilisé des colonnes pour soutenir la base métallique sur laquelle l'habitation est érigée.

Die Architekten benutzten stabile Säulen, um die Basis aus Metall zu halten, auf der das Haus konstruiert wurde.

The rooms on the top floor seek to eliminate any superfluous elements that would hinder the feeling of spaciousness.

Les pièces de l'étage supérieur ont été conçues en éliminant les éléments superflus qui pourraient gêner la sensation d'espace.

Bei der Planung der Räume im oberen Geschoss verzichtete man auf überflüssige Elemente, die den Eindruck von Weite stören könnten.

☐ Residence in Sydney
Résidence à Sydney
Wohnung in Sydney

Marsh Cashman Architects

The primary aim of this project was to provide a home for a major collection of books and contemporary art. The house is defined by a longitudinal composition dominated by right-angled forms that provide a support for the works on display. A fascinating interplay of juxtaposed forms, making up the fire-place, the various levels and a bridge on the top story, conjures up an interior space with a great formal richness. A dramatic effect is created by the layout and proportions of the library, occupying the total height of the space to give the impression of a structural wall made of books. On the ground level on the back of a house, a little patio with a swimming pool serves as an oasis of peace in the middle of the city, and at the same provides the whole level with cooling ventilation during the hot summer months.

L'objectif principal de cette maison est d'abriter une importante collection de livres et d'art contemporain. La demeure affiche une composition longitudinale, dominée par des formes en angle droit qui servent d'appui aux oeuvres exposées. Une fascinante interaction de formes juxtaposées, donnant forme à la cheminée, les différents niveaux et la passerelle du niveau supérieur, façonnent ensemble un espace intérieur d'une grande richesse formelle. Le design et les dimensions de la bibliothèque créent un effet théâtral. En effet, elle occupe la hauteur totale de l'espace, ce qui donne l'impression d'être devant un mur fait de livres. A l'arrière de l'habitation, au niveau du rez-de-chaussée, un petit patio doté d'une piscine, véritable havre de paix au cœur de la ville, permet à la fois de ventiler et de rafraîchir tout le niveau durant les mois de forte chaleur estivale.

Das Hauptziel bei der Planung dieser Wohnung war, eine umfassende Sammlung von Büchern und zeitgenössischer Kunst unterzubringen. Die Wohnung ist länglich geschnitten, und wird von rechtwinkligen Elementen beherrscht, die als Stützen für die ausgestellten Werke dienen. Die faszinierende Wechselwirkung zwischen den nebeneinander liegenden Formen, aus denen der Kamin, die verschiedenen Ebenen und eine Brücke in das obere Geschoss entstehen, lässt einen sehr formenreichen Raum entstehen. Die Gestaltung und die Größe lassen die Bibliothek geradezu dramatisch wirken. Sie nimmt den gesamten Raum in seiner Höhe ein, so dass der Eindruck entsteht, dass die tragende Wand aus Büchern besteht. Im hinteren Teil des Wohnhauses liegt ein kleiner Hof mit Swimmingpool, eine Oase des Friedens inmitten der Stadt, der auch gleichzeitig für die Belüftung und Kühlung während der heißen Sommermonate dient.

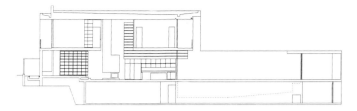

Longitudinal section Section longitudinale Längsschnitt

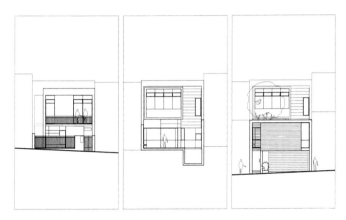

Elevations Élévations Aufrisse

First floor Premier étage Erstes Obergeschoss

Ground floor Rez-de-chaussée Erdgeschoss

Das Haus wird durch die längliche Komposition definiert, in der Formen mit rechten Winkeln vorherrschen.

La maison est définie par une composition longitudinale dominée par des formes aux angles droits.

The house is defined by a longitudinal composition dominated by right-angled forms.

The patio pool serves as a refreshing oasis on summer days and at the same time provides the house with a constant, cooling ventilation.

La piscine du patio sert d'oasis rafraîchissant les journées estivales tout en procurant à l'habitation une ventilation et une fraîcheur constantes.

Der Swimmingpool im Hof ist eine erfrischende Oase in den Sommermonaten und sorgt gleichzeitig für eine ständige Kühlung und Belüftung des Inneren.

Fong-Rodríguez House
Maison Fong-Rodríguez
Haus Fong-Rodríguez

Craig Steely Architecture

The client – a writer and journalist – wanted a flexible space in which to live, work and entertain that would respond to the site's stunning views and provide the feeling of being open to the exterior. The living area was placed on the top floor to enjoy the views of the city, while the middle floor has a flexible layout of bedrooms, a writing studio and gallery arranged around sliding cherry wood walls, a staircase with glass treads and two bathrooms with subtle color schemes. A stainless-steel rimmed circular opening in the roof measuring 8 ft. in diameter casts an oval of sunlight that moves as the day advances, like a huge sundial. All the materials used for the floor and walls are gray, setting off the chairs and kitchen closets, which are designed in explosive colors.

Le client, écrivain et journaliste, désirait un espace flexible où vivre, travailler et profiter des vues offertes par l'emplacement dans une atmosphère d'ouverture vers l'extérieur. La zone de séjour se situe à l'étage supérieur bénéficiant ainsi des vues sur la ville, tandis que l'étage intermédiaire est conçu de manière flexible avec chambres à coucher, studio et une galerie disposée autour de cloisons coulissantes en bois de cerisier, un escalier aux marches de verre et deux salles de bains. Une ouverture circulaire avec une monture d'acier inoxydable d'environ deux mètres et demi de diamètre, percée dans la toiture du balcon, laisse entrer un rayon de lumière solaire qui se déplace au fil de la journée, à l'instar d'un énorme cadran solaire. Les sols et les murs se déclinent dans des tonalités de gris, exaltant certains éléments de mobilier, à l'instar des sièges et des armoires de cuisine, conçus dans des couleurs explosives.

Der Kunde, ein Schriftsteller und Journalist, wünschte sich eine flexible Umgebung, in der er wohnen, arbeiten und den wundervollen Blick auf die schöne Umgebung genießen könnte. Der Wohnzimmerbereich liegt im oberen Stockwerk, von dem aus man den Blick auf die Stadt hat. Im flexibel gestalteten Zwischengeschoss liegen die Schlafzimmer, das Schreibzimmer und eine Galerie entlang einer Reihe von Schiebepaneelen aus Kirschbaum. Außerdem gibt es eine Treppe mit Stufen aus Glas und zwei Bäder in verschiedenen Farben. Ein Öffnung mit einer Fassung aus Edelstahl und einem Durchmesser von zweieinhalb Metern, der aus dem Dach des Balkons des oberen Stockwerks ausgeschnitten wurde, lässt das Sonnenlicht in ovaler Form einfallen, während der Tag fortschreitet, eine Art riesige Sonnenuhr. Die Boden- und Wand- materialien sind in Grautönen gehalten, während einige Elemente des Mobiliars wie Stühle und Küchenschränke in kräftigen Farben gestaltet sind.

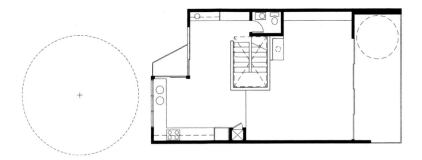

Second floor Deuxième étage Zweites Obergeschoss

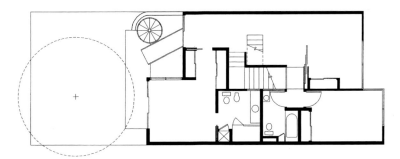

First floor Premier étage Erstes Obergeschoss

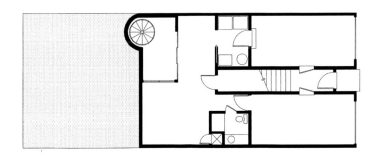

Ground floor Rez-de-chaussée Erdgeschoss

The terrace offers the stunning views of the entire city.

La terrasse permet de jouir de vues exceptionnelles sur toute la ville.

Von der Terrasse aus hat man einen wundervollen Blick auf die Stadt.

⌂
The façade represents the typical San Francisco postmodern style.

La façade représente le style post-moderne de San Francisco.

Die Fassade zeigt sich im typischen postmodernen Stil von San Francisco.

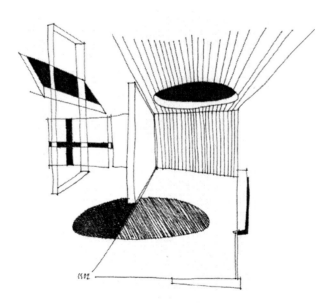

Sketch Esquisse Skizze

☐ Gillipsie/Airaghi

A+D Architecture

An "earthquake shack" produced made to accommodate victims of the 1906 earthquake was turned into a loft by modernizing its facilities and creating an open living space. The original house was transported to its present location in 1920 and placed on top of a basement. The architects took on the challenge of reinterpreting this model, raising the structure by one and a half stories and converting it into two residential apartments. The original wooden floors have been retained, while stacked double-height spaces have been connected to the old shack by a gallery that serves as a bridge between the old and the new. Old wooden furniture mingles with polished wood and stainless-steel surfaces. An interesting collection of artwork and furniture complements the diversity created by the varied yet disciplined use of materials and colors.

Une « maisonnette post-séisme » fabriquée pour abriter les victimes du tremblement de terre de 1906 a été transformée en loft en modernisant ses installations et créant un espace de vie ouvert. L'habitation d'origine, transportée à son emplacement actuel en 1920, a été posée au-dessus de fondations. Les architectes ont relevé le défi de revisiter ce modèle, en élevant la structure d'un étage et demi pour le convertir en deux appartements. Les sols de bois d'origine sont conservés, tandis que les espaces superposés sur deux hauteurs sont reliés à l'ancienne maisonnette grâce à une galerie servant de passerelle entre le passé et le présent. Le mobilier ancien en bois se mêle aux surfaces en bois vernis et en acier inoxydable. Une intéressante collection d'oeuvres d'art et de mobilier s'ajoute à la diversité ressortant de l'emploi varié, mais ordonné, de matériaux et couleurs.

Ein „Erdbebenhäuschen", wie sie in Massen produziert wurden, um die Opfer des Erdbebens von 1906 aufzunehmen, wurde durch die Modernisierung der Installationen in ein Loft verwandelt. Es entstand ein sehr offener Raum. Das Originalgebäude wurde 1920 zu seinem heutigen Standort transportiert und auf einem Fundament befestigt. Die Architekten sahen es als eine Herausforderung an, dieses Modell neu zu interpretieren. Sie erweiterten die Struktur um anderthalb Stockwerke und machten zwei Wohnungen daraus. Der Originalfußboden aus Holz blieb erhalten, und die gestapelten Räume doppelter Höhe wurden mit der ehemaligen Hütte über eine Galerie verbunden, die als Brücke zwischen dem Alten und dem Neuen dient. Die alten Holzmöbel wurden mit Oberflächen aus poliertem Holz und Edelstahl gemischt. Eine interessante Kunst- und Möbelsammlung dient als Ergänzung der Verschiedenartigkeit der verwendeten Materialien und Farben.

Plan Plan Grundriss

The original wooden floors have been retained, while double-height spaces have been connected to the old shack.

Les parquets originaux ont été conservés, et les espaces, superposés sur deux hauteurs, sont reliés à l'ancienne maisonnette.

Die originalen Holzböden blieben erhalten, während die gestapelten Räume doppelter Höhe mit der einstigen Hütte verbunden sind.

A gallery serves as a bridge between the old and the new part of the house.

Une galerie sert à la fois de passerelle entre l'ancienne et la nouvelle partie de l'habitation.

Eine Galerie dient als Brücke zwischen dem alten und dem neuen Teil des Hauses.

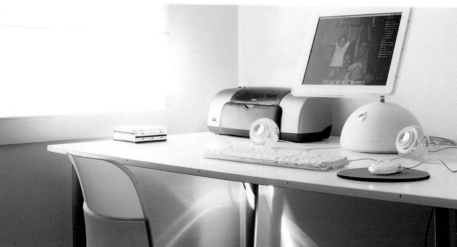

☐ Martin I

William Leddy / Leddy Maytum Stacey Architects

The client chose to establish his studio and residence inside a building located in a dense, semi-industrial area. To compensate for the constricted site, the primary aim of the project was to introduce as much light as possible into the living spaces. This was achieved in a number of ways: a glassed inner courtyard, slots between walls and skylights. The interior spaces are organized around a path integral to the building and used to move large canvases. Both the living and working spaces are characterized by surfaces in subdued tones and colorful objects, which combine to create a casual and light-hearted atmosphere. Stainless steel is the dominant material, present in both structural elements like the metal pillars and the surfaces in the kitchen and bathroom.

Un bâtiment situé dans une zone semi-industrielle trés dens densité a eté choisie par le client afin d'y installer son lieu de travail et de vie. Pour compenser l'étroitesse de l'emplacement, l'objectif essentiel du projet est de maximaliser l'apport de lumière dans les espaces de vie. A cet effet, diverses formules ont été envisagées : patio intérieur tout en verre, interstices entre les murs et lucarnes. Les espaces intérieurs s'articulent autour d'un parcours intégré à l'édifice permettant de déplacer de grandes toiles. Tant les zones de vie que les espaces de travail se déclinent dans des surfaces aux teintes douces et des objets colorés, associés pour créer une ambiance informelle et décontractée. L'acier inoxydable est la matière dominante, apparaissant sous formes d'éléments structurels, à l'instar de piliers métalliques ou comme revêtement de surface dans la cuisine et la salle de bains.

Diese Atelierwohnung wurde in einem bereits bestehenden Gebäude in einem dicht besiedelten, halb industriellen Viertel der Stadt geschaffen. Um die Enge des Grundstücks auszugleichen, versuchte man, soviel Licht wie möglich in die Wohnräume fallen zu lassen. Dazu wurden verschiedene Mittel eingesetzt. Eines davon ist der verglaste Innenhof und Schlitze zwischen den Wänden und Dachfenstern. Die Innenräume erstrecken sich entlang eines Wegs durch das Gebäude, der dazu benutzt wird, große Leinwände zu bewegen. Sowohl die Wohnals auch die Arbeitsräume haben Oberflächen in gedämpften Farben und sind mit bunten Objekten dekoriert, die eine legere und ungezwungene Atmosphäre entstehen lassen. Das dominierende Material ist Edelstahl, den man sowohl an den Strukturelementen wie an den Metallsäulen oder als Verkleidung der Oberflächen in Küche und Bad finden kann.

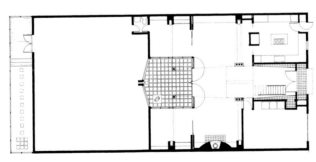

Plan Plan Grundriss

To compensate for the limited dimensions, the aim of the project was to introduce as much light as possible into the living spaces.

Pour compenser l'étroitesse de l'emplacement, l'objectif du projet a eté d'introduire le plus de lumière possible dans les zones de séjour.

Um die Enge des Grundstücks auszugleichen, versuchte man, soviel Licht wie möglich in die Wohnräume fallen zu lassen.

Subdued tones and colorful details were combined to create a casual and light-hearted atmosphere.

Les tons doux et les détails de couleur se conjuguent pour créer une ambiance informelle et décontractée.

Die gedämpften Töne und die farbigen Details wurden so kombiniert, dass eine lockere und leichte Atmosphäre entstand.

Layer House
Maison Layer
Layer Haus
Hiroaki Ohtani

This small house occupying a mere 355 sq. ft is located in the center of the city of Kobe. The structure is built like a trellis made of horizontal wood boards that alternate with empty spaces between them. The result is a room measuring 9 feet 4 inches wide by 25 feet deep. One of the advantages is the structure's horizontal arrangement, which allows diffused light to flow into the interior. There are several open areas inside that serve as fluid connections between the rooms, wich are are arranged on different levels according to their degree of intimacy; so, the public areas are near the entrance, while the private areas are behind them. These rooms are reached by a stairway with floating steps that project from the gaps in the trellis-like surrounding structure.

Cette petite maison qui n'occupe que 33 m2 de superficie est située au centre de la ville de Kobe. La structure s'élève à l'instar d'un espalier formé de barres de bois horizontales qui se succèdent alternativement en créant ainsi des couches vides. Le résultat fait apparaître une pièce de 2,88 m de large sur 7,7 m de long. Les vides horizontaux engendrés par la structure permettent à la lumière de pénétrer à l'intérieur de façon diffuse. L'intérieur offre diverses zones de distribution ouvertes créant une fluidité entre les divers espaces de vie. Les pièces se succèdent sur différents niveaux selon le degré d'intimité, afin que les zones publiques soient proches de l'accès, laissant derrière elles les zones privées, auxquelles on accède grâce à un escalier constitué de marches en saillie, disposées dans les espaces vides de la structure enveloppante.

Dieses kleine Haus nimmt eine Fläche von nur 33 m² in der Stadt Kobe ein. Die Struktur erhebt sich wie ein Spalier aus waagerechten Holzstangen, die übereinander angeordnet sind und freie Schichten formen. So entstand ein 2,88 m breiter und 7,7 m langer Raum. Die waagerechten freien Bereiche in der Struktur lassen das Tageslicht diffus in das Innere eindringen wo es mehrere offene Bereiche gibt aus denen sich fließend die verschiedenen Wohnumgebungen ergeben. Die Zimmer folgen einander auf verschiedenen Ebenen, je nachdem, wie privat sie genutzt werden. So liegen die öffentlichen Bereiche in Eingangsnähe, danach kommen die privateren Räume, die man über eine Treppe mit frei schwebenden Stufen erreicht, die sich in den ausgesparten Bereichen der umhüllenden Struktur befinden.

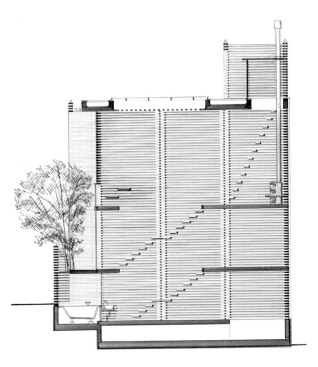

Section Section Schnitt

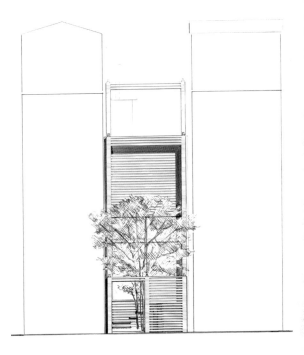

Elevation Élévation Aufriss

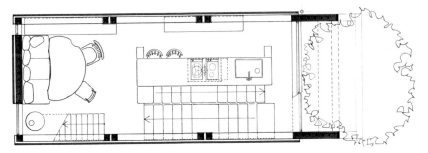

Plan Plan Grundriss

The structure of the house is built like a trellis made of horizontal wooden boards alternating with empty spaces.

La structure de l'habitation a été construite à l'instar d'un caillebotis fait de lattes de bois horizontales avec une alternance d'espaces vides entre elles.

Die Struktur des Hauses wurde wie ein Gitterwerk aus waagerechten Holztafeln konstruiert, zwischen denen sich Freiräume befinden.

Wood is the main material, used in the exterior structure and the façade, as well as in the furniture.

Le bois est le principal matériau utilisé sur la structure extérieure, sur la façade et pour le mobilier.

Holz ist das wichtigste Material, es wurde sowohl an der äußeren Struktur und der Fassade als auch für die Möbel verwendet.

Residence in Melbourne
Résidence à Melbourne
Residenz in Melbourne

John Wardle Architects

This project was designed to take advantage of every possible view, from the interior or the exterior of the house. The long, thin copper-clad structure gives rise to a succession of vistas, and the resulting volume provides an unusual interior layout. Thus, for instance, both the kitchen and the dining room are at the rear of the building, overlooking the city of Melbourne, while at the opposite end sweeping views of the neighbourhood are on offer. Subtle details in the spatial distribution strike up a relationship between the different rooms and levels within the home. Pale wooden floors add warmth and harmonize with the natural surroundings.

Ce projet a été envisagé sous l'angle de l'exploitation des vues possibles, tant celles qui s'obtiennent de l'intérieur de l'habitation que celles de l'habitation même. La structure allongée de la maison est recouverte de panneaux de cuivre qui créent une alternance de vues tout en formant un volume et un agencement intérieur inhabituels. A titre d'exemple, la cuisine et la salle à manger sont situées dans la partie postérieure de la maison, d'où l'on peut admirer les vues sur Melbourne. L'autre extrémité offre une vue panoramique sur la banlieue environnante. Des petits détails dans la distribution de l'espace instaurent différentes relations entre les pièces et les différents niveaux de la maison. Le parquet de bois clair dégage de la chaleur et s'harmonise à l'environnement naturel qui entoure la maison.

Bei der Planung dieses Hauses experimentierte man vor allem mit dem möglichen Ausblick, den man sowohl im Inneren des Hauses selbst als auch im Außenbereich hat. Die längliche Struktur wurde mit Kupferpaneelen verkleidet, die verschiedene Ausblicke ermöglichen und im Inneren eine untypische Form und Anordnung entstehen lassen. So befinden sich zum Beispiel die Küche und das Esszimmer im hinteren Teil des Hauses, von dem aus man einen Blick über Melbourne hat. Auf der gegenüberliegenden Seite blickt man auf die nahegelegenen Vororte. Kleine Einzelheiten in der Raumaufteilung lassen verschiedene Beziehungen zwischen den einzelnen Räumen und Ebenen des Hauses entstehen. Der Boden aus hellem Holz lässt die Wohnung klar und warm wirken und harmoniert mit der umgebenden Natur.

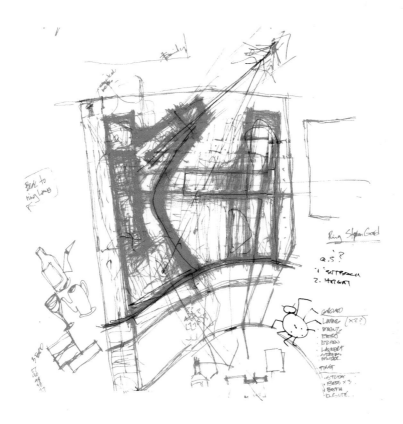

Ground floor Rez-de-chaussée Erdgeschoss

First floor Premier étage Erstes Obergeschoss

A white concrete path leads from the rear to the entrance, running alongside the house.

Un sentier de béton blanc longe la maison en partant de l'arrière pour aller jusqu'à l'entrée.

Ein Pfad aus weißem Beton führt vom hinteren Teil des Hauses entlang zum Eingang.

In order to create a succession of views, the large structure was wrapped in bands of copper.

Pour créer une alternance de vues, la grande structure a été parée de bandes de cuivre.

Um wechselnde Ausblicke zu schaffen, wurde die große Struktur mit Kupferstreifen verkleidet.

The whole rear of the house is made of huge glass windows, looking out toward the nearby suburbs.

Toute la partie arrière de l'habitation est constituée de grandes baies vitrées, donnant sur la banlieue proche.

Der gesamte hintere Teil des Hauses hat große Fenster, von denen aus man auf die nahegelegenen Vororte sieht.

The dining room is situated in the rear of the house, which enjoys a view of the city.

La salle à manger, située à l'arrière de l'habitation, offre des vues sur la ville.

Das Speisezimmer befindet sich im hinteren Teil der Wohnung, von dem aus man auf die Stadt blickt.

☐ House in Durgerdam
Maison à Durgerdam
Haus in Durgerdam

Moriko Kira

This project involved the restoration of a traditional house set on the Durgerdam dike. The addition of an annex with the kitchen and dining area sets up a dynamic relationship between this new space and the main house, which are linked by a small patio. The new addition features finishes such as stainless steel and glass combined with wood. By linking the new structure to the main house with a single staircase, the architects managed to create an intermediate patio that allows natural light to flow through either side of the kitchen. The extension highlights the transition between the façade and the rear of the house, creating a sequence of different spaces. The bathroom, bedroom, patio, new kitchen and living room are characterised by their varying relationships with the surrounding landscape.

Ce projet concerne la restauration d'une maison traditionnelle située sur la digue de Durgerdam. Une structure indépendante, annexée à l'habitation principale, accueille une cuisine et un séjour, créant ainsi une relation dynamique entre les deux volumes, reliés par un petit patio. L'agrandissement affiche des finitions réalisées en matériaux, tels l'acier inoxydable et le verre associé au bois. En reliant la nouvelle structure à l'habitation principale par un escalier, les architectes ont créé un patio intermédiaire permettant à la lumière naturelle de pénétrer la cuisine. L'extension renforce la transition entre la façade et l'arrière de la maison tout en créant une enfilade d'espaces. La salle de bains, la chambre à coucher, le patio, la nouvelle cuisine et le séjour se définissent en fonction des diverses relations qu'ils établissent avec le paysage environnant.

Dieses Bauprojekt bestand aus der Renovierung eines typischen Hauses am Deich Durgerdam. Eine unabhängige Struktur wurde hinzugefügt, in der sich die Küche und das Wohnzimmer befinden, wobei eine dynamische Beziehung zwischen beiden Formen entstand, die über einen kleinen Hof miteinander verbunden sind. Der Anbau ist mit Oberflächen aus modernem Material wie Edelstahl und Glas in Kombination mit Holz gestaltet. Durch die Verbindung der neuen Struktur mit der Hauptwohnung über eine Treppe entstand ein Innenhof, durch den Tageslicht in die Küche fällt. Der Anbau unterstreicht den Übergang von der Fassade zum hinteren Teil des Hauses und schafft eine Sequenz von Räumen. Das Badezimmer, das Schlafzimmer, der Hof, die neue Küche und das Wohnzimmer zeichnen sich durch die verschiedenartigen Beziehungen aus, die zu der umgebenden Landschaft entstanden sind.

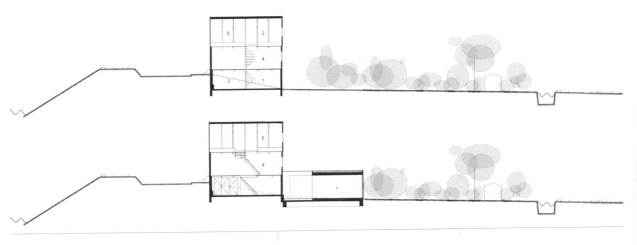

Sections Sections Schnitte

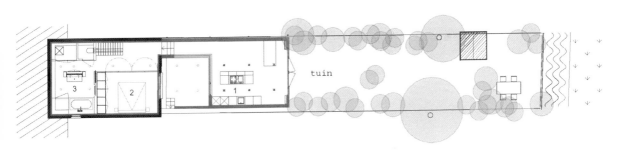

tuin

Plan Plan Grundriss

The new kitchen is characterized by its direct relationship with the surrounding landscape.

La nouvelle cuisine est en relation directe avec le paysage environnant.

Die neue Küche ist durch die direkte Beziehung zu der umliegenden Landschaft gekennzeichnet.

The white roof structure combines with the wooden flooring to create a warm and friendly atmosphere.

La structure blanche du plafond ainsi que les sols boisés créent une ambiance chaude et agréable.

Die Struktur des weißen Daches schafft in Kombination mit den Holzböden eine warme und angenehme Atmosphäre.

☐ Elektra House
Maison Elektra
Haus Elektra

David Adjaye

While the house's contemporary appearance is the result of the materials and formal language used, the building is totally integrated with the neighboring houses. The architect's concept was to build a house within a house, in order to take advantage of the existing elements. The new building uses the foundations and outer walls of the former structure, but a new metal framework was inserted in the interior, to create an upper floor, which is used as a sleeping area. The façades are suspended from the metal structure, minimizing the load on the existing foundations. The façade's lack of ostentation is reflected in the interior, where a two-story space with a skylight runs the entire length of the house. This space provides pools of sunlight for the flexible area used as living or work space.

Si les matériaux et le langage formel utilisés confèrent à l'habitation son allure contemporaine, celle-ci s'intègre parfaitement au paysage environnant. Le concept initial propose la construction d'une maison dans une maison pour tirer parti au maximum des éléments existants avant de réaliser le projet. La nouvelle habitation tire parti des fondations de l'ancienne structure ainsi que des murs d'enceinte. Un nouveau cadre métallique, intégré à l'intérieur, forme la toiture de tous les espaces, tout en créant un étage supérieur, qui sert de chambre à coucher. Les façades se détachent de l'ossature métallique, générant une charge minimale sur les fondations préexistantes. Le manque d'expression de la façade se traduit à l'intérieur par un espace à double hauteur doté d'une lucarne continue sur toute la longueur de la maison. Cet espace fait office de puits de lumière solaire dans la zone polyvalente, servant d'espace de vie ou de lieu de travail.

Obwohl die verwendeten Materialien und Formen das Haus sehr modern aussehen lassen, fügt es sich perfekt in die Umgebung ein. Der Ausgangspunkt der Planung war, ein Haus im Haus zu errichten, um die bereits vorhandenen Elemente so weit wie möglich auszunutzen. Für den neuen Bau benutzte man das Fundament des alten Hauses und die Außenmauern. Ein neuer Metallrahmen wurde in das Innere eingefügt und dient als Decke für alle Räume, so dass ein oberes Stockwerk entstanden ist, in dem sich das Schlafzimmer befindet. Die Fassaden hängen an der Metallstruktur, so dass die existierenden Fundamente kaum belastet werden. Die Ausdruckslosigkeit der Fassade wird im Inneren zu einem zweistöckigen Raum mit einem Dachfenster, das am ganzen Haus entlang verläuft. Dieser Raum stellt eine Art Solarkamin für den flexiblen Bereich dar, der als Wohn- oder Arbeitszimmer benutzt werden kann.

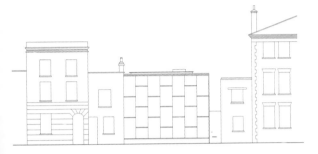

Elevation Élévation Aufriss

Section Section Schnitt

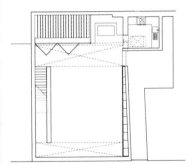

Ground floor Rez-de-chaussée Erdgeschoss

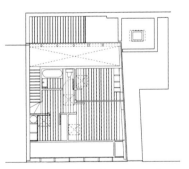

First floor Premier étage Erstes Obergeschoss

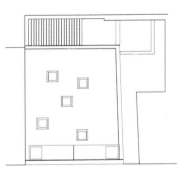

Roof plan Plan du toit Dachgeschoss

The façades are suspended from the metal structure, minimizing the load on the existing foundations.

Les façades sont suspendues à la structure métallique, atténuant ainsi la charge sur les fondations existantes.

Die Fassaden hängen an der Metallstruktur und verringern so die Belastung des existierenden Fundamentes.

This project goes away from the traditional idea of illuminating a room and the reflection, brightness, and movement of light become real experiences in the interior.

Ce projet s'éloigne de l'idée traditionnelle d'éclairage d'une pièce et le reflet, l'éclat et le mouvement de la lumière se métamorphosent en véritables expériences intérieures.

Bei diesem Projekt wird hingegen den traditionellen Konzepten der Beleuchtung mit Wiederspiegelungen und bewegtem Licht experimentiert.

☐ Villa Slit

C. Matsuba / Tele-design

In Japan, small scale housing is becoming popular, as illustrated by this home with only 721 sq. ft located in a densely populated residential area in Tokyo. The kitchen and dining areas are on the ground floor, while the living area is on the second level. The top floor is reserved for the bedroom and a terrace. A system of bamboo screens cover the façade and create an entertaining and ever changing exterior. The translucent quality of this material, which is also present in the interior, establishes a visual connection between the different spaces in the house and at the same time provides the necessary privacy from the outside. The very sensitive and esthetic design makes use of traditional materials and a modern design approach, to combine the natural heritage with the contemporary spirit of daily life.

Au Japon, la petite échelle est à son apogée, comme l'illustre cette habitation de 67 m² seulement, située dans une zone résidentielle de Tokyo, à forte densité de population. Le rez-de-chaussée accueille la cuisine et la salle à manger, alors que le deuxième étage héberge le salon. Le dernier étage est réservé à la chambre à coucher et à la terrasse. Un système de persiennes en bambou couvre la façade en configurant un extérieur amusant, qui change constamment. La translucidité de cette matière, également présente à l'intérieur, établit un lien visuel entre les divers espaces formant la résidence tout en lui conférant l'intimité nécessaire vis-à-vis de l'extérieur. Ce projet, d'une haute sensibilité esthétique, associe des matériaux traditionnels à un design contemporain, conjuguant l'héritage naturel à l'esprit actuel de la vie quotidienne.

In Japan gewinnen die Wohnungen im kleinen Maßstab zunehmend an Bedeutung. Das beweist auch diese Wohnung auf nur 67 m² in einem Wohnviertel im dicht besiedelten Tokio. Im Erdgeschoss liegen die Küche und das Speisezimmer und im ersten Stock das Wohnzimmer. Im zweiten Stock befinden sich das Schlafzimmer und die Terrasse. Ein System aus Bambusjalousien bedeckt die Fassade und schafft so ein interessantes, sich ständig veränderndes Äußeres. Dieses Material ist lichtdurchlässig, und auch im Inneren wurden durchscheinende Materialien verwendet, so dass eine visuelle Verbindung zwischen den verschiedenen Bereichen des Hauses entsteht, aber gleichzeitig der notwendige Schutz der Intimsphäre gewährleistet wird. An diesem unter ästhetischen Gesichtspunkten sehr gelungenen Haus wurden traditionelle Materialien mit einem zeitgenössischen Design kombiniert. So integrierte man das natürliche Erbe mit dem modernen Geist des täglichen Lebens.

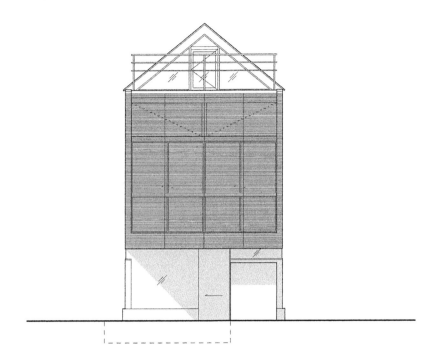

Elevation Élévation Aufriss

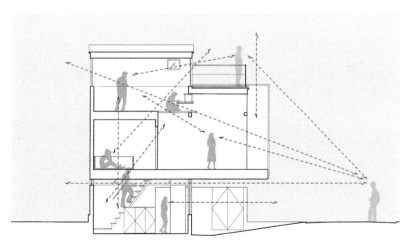

Section Section Schnitt

The material's semi-transparency creates a visual link between the interior and the exterior.

La semi-transparence du matériau instaure un lien visuel entre l'intérieur et l'extérieur.

Die halbe Transparenz des Materials schafft eine visuelle Verbindung zwischen Innen und Außen.

A combination of modern and traditional materials like wood, steel, and bamboo reflect the contemporary trend of Japanese architecture.

Une association de matériaux modernes et traditionnels tels le bois, l'acier et le bambou, reflète la tendance contemporaine de l'architecture japonaise.

Eine Kombination von modernen und traditionellen Materialien wie Holz, Stahl und Bambus spiegelt den zeitgenössischen Trend in der japanischen Architektur wider.

☐ Lina House
Maison Lina
Linahaus

Caramel Architekten

This unit, originally conceived as a small extension to a family house, is in fact completely autonomous and contains all the services required for a self-contained home. The limited floor space, coupled with financial restrictions, determined what type of construction was possible, and it was finally decided to design a module that could easily be removed or enlarged in the future. A glass wall floods the interior space with light, as well as opening it to the exterior — a wooded area on the grounds of the house. White is the predominant color inside the house, endowing it with a continuity that is broken only by dashes of color on the furnishings and in the bathroom. The floor is made of pale wood throughout the house, adding warmth to the setting.

Cette unité, conçue au départ comme une petite extension de maison individuelle, contient, en fait, tous les services indispensables pour être entièrement autonome. Les limites de la surface habitable alliées aux contraintes budgétaires ont déterminé le type de construction, à savoir un module facile à éliminer ou à agrandir ultérieurement. Une immense baie vitrée inonde l'espace intérieur de lumière naturelle tout en l'ouvrant sur l'extérieur, une zone boisée du terrain. Le blanc donne le ton dans toute la maison, lui conférant une continuité que seules les touches de couleur du mobilier et de la salle de bains osent interrompre. Le bois clair, qui recouvre le sol de toute la maison, y dégage une ambiance chaleureuse.

Diese Wohneinheit, die anfangs nur ein kleiner Anbau an ein Einfamilienhaus werden sollte, ist vollständig autonom und verfügt über alle notwendigen Funktionen, um darin unabhängig zu wohnen. Die Bauweise wurde durch die nur begrenzt zur Verfügung stehende, bebaubaren Fläche und das beschränkte Budget bestimmt, so dass man ein Modul plante, das man leicht wieder abbauen oder erweitern könnte. Durch eine Glaswand dringt reichlich Licht ins Innere und die Wohnung öffnet sich nach draußen zu einem kleinen Wald. In der Wohnung herrscht die Farbe Weiß vor, was die Wohnung fließend wirken lässt. Nur die Möbel und das Bad unterbrechen dieses Weiß mit kleinen Farbtupfern. Der Boden im gesamten Haus ist aus hellem Holz, das eine sehr warme Wohnatmosphäre schafft.

The large glass wall opens the home on to the exterior and allows sunshine to enter, making the most of the daylight hours.

L'immense baie vitrée ouvre l'habitation sur l'extérieur, permettant à la lumière naturelle de pénétrer l'espace et de profiter au maximum de l'ensoleillement.

Durch die große Glaswand, die die Wohnung nach außen öffnet und Tageslicht eindringen lässt, werden die Sonnenstunden maximal genutzt.

The wooden floor adds warmth, while the predominance of pale colors conveys a sense of calm and harmony.

Le parquet ajoute une note de chaleur à la maison où la prédominance de couleurs pales confère une atmosphère de calme et d'harmonie.

Der Holzboden schafft eine warme und gemütliche Wohnatmosphäre, in der helle Farben dominieren, die Ruhe und Harmonie vermitteln.

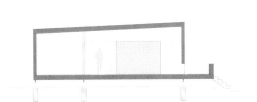

Section Section Schnitt

Plan Plan Grundriss

☐ **Valls House**

Maison Valls

Vallshaus

Rob Dubois

This house is located in the historic center of the town, characterized by its low buildings with an interior patio or garden. The restricted budget and the limited capacities of the available local contractors obliged the architect to stick to traditional technical and material solutions in order to keep the schedule and costs in check, and also to guarantee that the building will last without any great maintenance problems. The house is closed on the north side facing the street and opens on to a garden on the south side. The main areas — living room, two bedrooms, and study — have high ceiling (11 ft). The service areas — kitchen and main bathroom — are 8 ft high. Rather than viewing these lofty dimensions as a hindrance, the architect took advantage of them to create a number of multifunctional spaces.

Cette habitation est située dans le centre historique de la ville, une zone caractérisée par des édifices de faible hauteur, dotés de patio intérieur ou de jardin. Le budget étriqué et les possibilités limitées des entrepreneurs de la zone ont contraint l'architecte à pencher pour les techniques et matériaux traditionnels, afin d'assouplir le processus de construction, baisser les prix et garantir la durabilité du projet sans trop intervenir dans son essence. Ce qui a abouti à la conception d'une maison fermée côté nord donnant sur la rue, et qui s'ouvre au jardin, côté sud. Les zones principales, salle à manger, chambre et bureau, jouissent d'une hauteur considérable de 3,40 m, contrairement aux zones de service – cuisine et salle de bains principale –, où les plafonds font 2,40 m de hauteur. Au lieu de considérer ces dimensions comme un obstacle, l'architecte les a exploitées pour créer des espaces multifonctionnels.

Dieses Haus befindet sich in der historischen Stadtmitte, einem Viertel voller niedriger Gebäude mit Garten oder Innenhof. Aufgrund des beschränkten Budgets und der begrenzten Möglichkeiten der Bauunternehmer in diesem Gebiet war der Architekt dazu gezwungen, traditionelle Techniken und Materialien einzusetzen, um den Bauprozess zu beschleunigen, die Kosten zu senken und die Haltbarkeit zu sichern, ohne dass dabei zu viele Kosten für die Instandhaltung anfallen. So entwarf er ein Haus, das auf seiner zur Straße hin liegenden Nordseite geschlossen ist und sich zu dem Garten im Süden öffnet. Die wichtigsten Bereiche wie das Esszimmer, die beiden Schlafzimmer und das Atelier sind relativ hoch, 3,40 m, und die funktionellen Räume, also die Küche und das große Badezimmer haben 2,40 m hohe Decken. Anstatt diese Maße als ein Hindernis anzusehen, hat der Architekt sie genutzt, um multifunktionelle Räume zu schaffen.

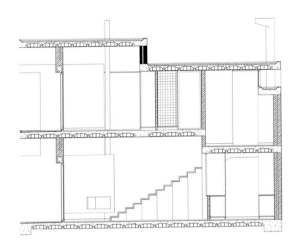

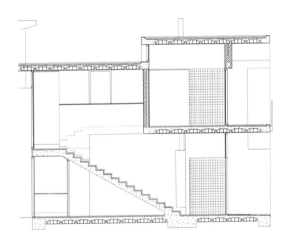

Sections Sections Schnitte

The house is reminiscent of the heroic era of modern architecture, particularly one of the construction models of the early thirties in Vienna.

L'habitation est une réminiscence de l'époque héroïque de l'architecture moderne, un des modèles de construction du début des années trente à Vienne.

Die Wohnung erinnert an die heroische Zeit der modernen Architektur, sie ist ein Beispiel für die Bauweise zu Beginn der Dreißigerjahre in Wien.

The main concept behind the house is the creation of a sense of openness and of spaces interrelated to each other.

Le concept premier de l'habitation est de créer une sensation d'ouverture et d'interaction spatiale.

Das wichtigste Konzept bei der Planung war es, die Wohnung offen zu gestalten und die Räume miteinander zu verbinden.

☐ P·O·M Ebisu

Nishimori Architect & Associates

This small-scale house has special functions as an urban-style second house, as the owner planned to use it for his business base in the urban core of Tokyo, as a complement to his main house in the suburbs. The irregular shape of the lot made it impossible to base the program on rectangular spaces if the ground area was to be exploited to the maximum. To solve this problem, the area was divided into two triangles, with three walls in a diagonal line from front to back, creating bigger and smaller spaces side by side. Each of the floors has its own function, as a meeting area, office space or living quarters. The meeting space on the first floor is not just for the owner's private use; it is also rented out. Therefore, the approach through the entrance needed to be as open and as bright as possible, even though this space faces a narrow alley in the residential block.

Cette petite construction affiche un programme multifonctionnel, puisque le propriétaire avait besoin d'une deuxième résidence au centre de Tokyo qui soit aussi son lieu de travail. Le terrain de forme irrégulière ne permettait pas au programme de se baser sur des formes rectangulaires pour optimaliser la surface au sol. Ce problème a été résolu en divisant l'espace en deux triangles, avec trois murs en diagonal allant d'un extrême à l'autre. La juxtaposition d'espaces larges et étroits fait que les pièces paraissent plus grandes. Ainsi, chacun des trois étages qui la compose a une fonction : habitation, bureau et salle de réunion. Cette dernière, en plus d'être utilisée par le propriétaire, peut être louée : à ce titre, l'accès se doit d'être diaphane et ouvert, même si cette partie donne sur un étroit passage. L'escalier, qui se projette vers la rue, relie les trois étages entre eux et permet de les percevoir comme un espace ouvert.

Dieses kleine Gebäude enthält multifunktionelle Räume, weil der Eigentümer einen zweiten Wohnsitz im Zentrum Tokios benötigt, an dem er auch arbeiten kann. Das Grundstück ist unregelmäßig geformt. Deshalb konnte man sich bei der Planung nicht auf rechteckige Formen berufen, wenn man die Fläche maximal nutzen wollte. Um dieses Problem zu lösen, wurde der Raum in zwei Dreiecke unterteilt, die drei diagonale Wände von einer Seite zur anderen haben. Das Nebeneinanderstellen von weiten und engen Räumen lässt die Zimmer größer wirken. Jedes der drei Stockwerke hat eine Funktion: Wohnung, Büro und Konferenzzimmer. Dieses wird nicht nur vom Besitzer benutzt, sondern auch vermietet. Deshalb musste der Zugang dazu transparent und offen sein, obwohl er in einer engen Gasse liegt. Die Treppe, die zur Straße liegt, verbindet die drei Etagen und lässt sie wie einen offenen Raum wirken.

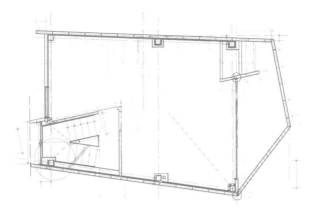

Second floor Deuxième étage Zweites Obergeschoss

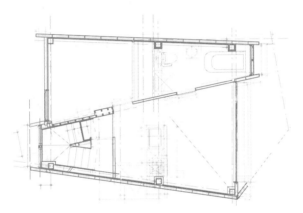

First floor Premier étage Erstes Obergeschoss

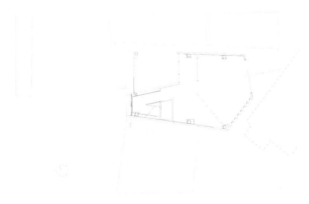

Ground floor Rez-de-chaussée Erdgeschoss

The house creates the illusion that the big spaces are bigger, and the smaller ones, even smaller.

L'habitation génère l'illusion d'agrandir les espaces déjà grands et de réduire encore plus les petits espaces par rapport à la réalité.

Die Wohnung schafft die Illusion, dass die großen Räume noch größer und die kleinen noch kleiner wirken, als sie wirklich sind.

The staircase, which heads toward the street, connects the various areas, creating the impression that the home is open on all sides.

L'escalier, qui se projette vers la rue, relie divers espaces entre eux, créant l'illusion visuelle d'ouverture omniprésente dans l'habitation.

Die Treppe, die zur Straße liegt, verbindet verschiedene Räume und schafft den visuellen Eindruck, dass der gesamte Wohnraum sehr offen ist.

☐ Mini House
Mini maison
Minihaus

Atelier Bow Bow

Located within a dense residential district in the heart of the city, this home is very small, like many of Tokyo's architectural sites. In response to this fluid and unstable environment, the architects approached the project with the spatial limitations in mind and so left the lower volumes open to borders of the lot, creating a thin, steel structure that takes full advantage of the perimeter walls and floors of the building, dispensing with pillars and a beam framework. Stone steps lead to the entrance located at the side of the house, from where the three floors are visible. The basement floor consists of a storage room and a bedroom. On the ground floor, the entrance leads to a living room and kitchen on the left and a bathroom on the right. Upstairs, the first floor contains the main bedroom, and two small balconies on the front and side.

Située dans un quartier résidentiel à forte densité de popula- tion, au coeur d'une zone très urbaine, cette habitation, à l'ima- ge des espaces architecturaux de Tokyo, est très petite. Face à cet environnement fluide et instable, les architectes ont revisi- té l'édifice en fonction des limites de l'emplacement et laissé les volumes inférieurs ouverts jusqu'aux confins du terrain, créant une structure sur trois hauteurs aux visages multiples. La mince structure d'acier utilise pleinement les murs du péri- mètre et les sols de l'édifice, supprimant les colonnes principa- les et les structures des poutres. Des marches en pierre mènent à l'entrée située sur le côté de la maison, d'où l'on voit les trois étages. Le sous-sol comporte une pièce de rangement et une chambre à coucher. Au rez-de-chaussée, l'entrée mène à un salon et à une cuisine sur la gauche, la salle de bains se situant sur la droite. L'étage accueille la chambre à coucher principale, et deux petits balcons sur la façade avant et latérale.

Auf dieses inmitten eines dicht besiedelten Wohnviertels in einer sehr städtischen Zone gelegene Haus in Tokio trifft vor allem eine Beschreibung zu, nämlich dass es sehr klein ist. Als Antwort auf die sich ständig ändernde Umgebung haben die Architekten ein Gebäude entworfen, das an den Begrenzungen des Grundstücks beginnt und dessen Formen ohne Barrieren bis zu den Grundstücksgrenzen reichen. So entstand eine dreistö- ckige und sehr vielseitige Struktur. Die schlanke Stahlstruktur nutzt die Außenmauern und die Böden des Gebäudes vollstän- dig aus, so dass die Hauptsäulen und die Trägerstrukturen über- flüssig wurden. Steinstufen führen zum seitlichen Eingang, von dem aus man die drei Stockwerke sehen kann. Im Unterge- schoss liegen ein Lagerraum und ein Schlafzimmer. Im Erdge- schoss führt der Eingang zu einem Wohnzimmer und einer Küche auf der linken, und einem Badezimmer auf der rechten Seite. Im ersten Stock befindet sich das Hauptschlafzimmer und zwei kleine Balkone an der Vorder- und Seitenfassade.

Imagination and practicality is required when designing a small living space. Here, a staircase doubles as a shelf unit.

La conception d'un espace habitable réduit requiert une dose d'imagination et de sens pratique. Ici, l'escalier fait aussi fonction d'étagère.

Man muss bei der Gestaltung eines kleinen Wohnraums die Phantasie und das Gespür für das Praktische einsetzen. In diesem Fall dient die Treppe auch als Regal.

Large windows punctuate the walls, and inside the walls are used for storage, keeping the rooms remarkably uncluttered despite the limited space available.

Les grandes fenêtres ponctuent les murs et, à l'intérieur, les murs servent de zones de rangement, maintenant ainsi les pièces assez dépouillées, en dépit de l'espace disponible réduit.

Die großen Fenster sind über die Wände verteilt. Im Inneren werden die Wände als Lagerraum benutzt, so dass die Räume relativ leer sind, obwohl so wenig Platz zur Verfügung steht.

☐ Laidley House
Maison Laidley
Haus Laidley

Anne Fougeron

The intention behind this conversion was to unify the existing facade while creating several ways of guiding light into the interior spaces. The intervention focused on the front five feet of the structure. The one-dimensional nature of the house was transformed into a dialogue of transparent and solid layers, with strips of glazing in between. A skylight integrated into the new exterior concrete structure casts light on to the dining area inside. The protruding window stretching vertically up the facade defines the double-height void inside the house. The lower level consists of the living area, while the mezzanine overlooking it contains the bedroom. An effort was made to ensure that the materials and the finishes were related to the style of the surrounding buildings.

Ce projet de restauration effectué à vise à unifier la façade existante, en créant en même temps diverses façons de guider la lumière vers les espaces intérieurs. L'action entreprise est axée sur le centre avant de la structure. La nature unidimensionnelle de l'habitation s'est transformée en un dialogue de couches transparentes et opaques dotées de franges de verre intermédiaires. Une lucarne intégrée à la nouvelle structure extérieure en béton apporte la lumière à la salle à manger. La fenêtre en saillie, qui s'étend verticalement vers le haut de la façade, définit le vide sur deux hauteurs au sein de l'habitation. Le niveau inférieur comprend le séjour sur lequel donne un entresol avec la chambre à coucher. Ce projet traduit la volonté de mettre en relation les matériaux et les finitions avec le style des édifices avoisinants.

Bei diesem Umbau war das Ziel, die existierende Fassade zu vereinheitlichen und gleichzeitig verschiedene Formen zu schaffen, die das Tageslicht in die Innenräume leiten. Der Eingriff konzentrierte sich auf die anderthalb Meter vor der Struktur. Der eindimensionale Charakter dieses Hauses wurde zu einem Dialog zwischen transparenten und lichtundurchlässigen Schichten, zwischen denen verglaste Streifen liegen. Ein Dachfenster in der neuen Außenstruktur aus Beton lässt Licht in das Esszimmer fallen. Das Fenster, das herausragt, streckt sich vertikal über die Fassade hinaus und schafft den Hohlraum für die doppelte Höhe innerhalb der Wohnung. Auf der unteren Ebene liegt das Wohnzimmer, im Zwischengeschoss ein Schlafzimmer. Den Architekten ist es ausgezeichnet gelungen, Materialien und Oberflächen auszuwählen, die eine Beziehung zum Stil der angrenzenden Gebäude schaffen.

The protruding window stretching vertically up the facade defines the double-height void inside the house.

La fenêtre en saillie, qui s'étend à la verticale vers le haut de la façade, définit le vide sur deux hauteurs à l'intérieur de l'habitation.

Das Fenster, das herausragt, streckt sich vertikal über die Fassade hinaus und schafft den Hohlraum für die doppelte Höhe innerhalb der Wohnung.

The lower level of the house consists of the living area, while the mezzanine overlooking it contains the bedroom.

Le niveau inférieur de l'habitation représente la zone de séjour. L'entresol, qui donne sur ce dernier, héberge la chambre à coucher.

Auf der unteren Ebene liegt das Wohnzimmer, im Zwischengeschoss ein Schlafzimmer.

☐ Grandview Residence
Résidence Grandview
Residenz Grandview

Levy Art & Architecture

This residence, with a sculptural, highly worked mass running along the building's main facade, was determined by the architects' response to its location between a box building some fifty years old and some recently completed contemporary homes. The forms of the adjacent building were subtly incorporated, while adapting to the typical front-porch layout. The project involved the addition of a new bedroom, bathroom, lounge, deck and rooftop garden to an existing garage structure. The bedroom was placed next to the new living area as an open suite, while folding doors provide the option of converting the bedroom into a dark cocoon for sleeping. The walls are painted in bright colors, while the flooring is in earthy colors, bouncing around the natural light that comes in through the terrace doors.

Cette résidence, dont le volume sculptural très travaillé parcourt la façade principale de l'édifice dans le sens de la longueur, a été réalisée par les architectes en fonction de sa situation entre un édifice construit cinquante ans auparavant et une série d'habitations de facture récente. Les formes de l'édifice limitrophe s'intègrent avec subtilité, tout en s'adaptant au design typique du porche frontal. Le projet ajoute de nouveaux éléments, à l'instar de chambre à coucher, salle de bains, salon, plafond et un jardin dans la terrasse à une structure de garage existant. La chambre suite à coucher est adjacente au nouveau séjour, où les portes en accordéon permettent de transformer ladite chambre en un refuge sombre pour dormir. Les murs sont peints en couleurs vives et les sols sont dotés de tons couleur terre, réfléchissant la lumière naturelle qui pénètre par les portes de la terrasse.

Dieses Haus, das sich durch eine fein gearbeitete skulpturelle Form auszeichnet, die an der Hauptfassade des Gebäudes entlang verläuft, wurde von seiner Lage zwischen einem kastenförmigen Gebäude aus den Fünfzigerjahren und einer Reihe zeitgenössischer Wohnhäuser mit moderner Fassade bestimmt. Die Formen der angrenzenden Gebäude wurden subtil einbezogen, ebenso die typische Form der vorderen Veranda. Bei der Planung wurden ein neues Schlafzimmer, ein Bad, ein Wohnzimmer, ein Dach und eine Dachterrasse, die einer bereits existierenden Garage hinzugefügt wurde, miteinander verbunden. Das Schlafzimmer liegt direkt am neuen Wohnzimmer, so dass eine offene Suite entstand, von der man das Schlafzimmer mithilfe von Falttüren abtrennen kann. Die Wände sind in kräftigen Farben gestrichen, die Böden in Erdtönen gehalten. Das Licht, das durch die Terrassentüren fällt, wird gleichmäßig verteilt.

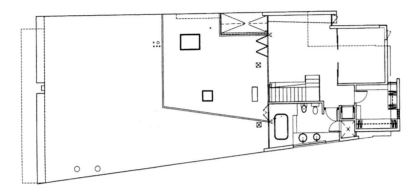

Second floor Deuxième étage Zweites Obergeschoss

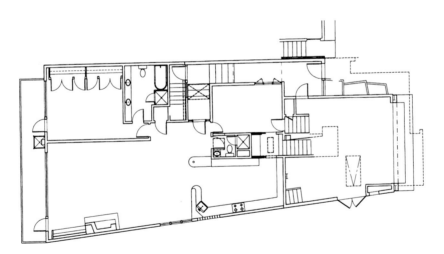

First floor Premier étage Erstes Obergeschoss

The sculptural form of the house is defined by the combination of a box building some fifty years old and a recently completed contemporary home.
La forme sculpturale de l'habitation est définie par un mélange entre un édifice du genre boîte datant d'une cinquantaine d'années et une habitation de facture récente.
Die skulpturelle Form der Wohnung wird durch eine Mischung aus einem kastenförmigen Gebäude aus den Fünfzigerjahren und einem zeitgenössischen Neubau definiert.

The folding doors provide the option of converting the bedroom into a dark cocoon for sleeping.

Les portes en accordéon permettent de transformer la chambre à coucher en refuge sombre pour dormir.

Die faltbaren Türen machen es möglich, das Schlafzimmer in einen dunklen Zufluchtsort zu verwandeln.

Magnolia Row

David Baker & Partners

The West Clawson area, long populated by artists, is home to a varied, highly creative community that has established itself in lofts and studios. This project, one of a series of townhouses, is a cross between an urban loft and a residential home. Open living areas span the main floor, with open-riser wooden stairways linking these to the more private bedrooms. The open-plan kitchen is equipped with stainless steel gas stoves, granite counters and maple closets. Hydronic heating, energy-efficient water heaters and state-of-the-art electronic equipment mean that these townhouses are not only well designed but also ecologically and technologically advanced. The big variety of forms, finishes and materials makes each room and area spatially and functionally distinct.

La zone de West Clawson, habitée depuis des lustres par des artistes, est le lieu de résidence d'une grande communauté très créative, installée dans des lofts et studios. Ce projet, d'une série de maisons individuelles, est un mélange entre un loft urbain et une habitation résidentielle. Les espaces de vie ouverts occupent l'étage principal et sont unis aux zones plus privées des chambres à coucher par des escaliers en bois, dotés d'une contremarche ouverte. La cuisine ouverte est équipée d'une cuisinière à gaz en acier inoxydable, un plan de travail en granit et des armoires en érable. Le système de chauffage hydraulique, les chauffe-eau à gain d'énergie et les équipements électroniques de pointe montrent que ces maisons sont non seulement bien conçues, mais qu'elles s'inscrivent aussi dans le progrès écologique et technologique. La grande variété de formes, finitions et matériaux convertit chaque espace en une zone différente tant sur le plan spatial que fonctionnel.

Das Viertel West Clawson war immer schon ein Wohnviertel für Künstler, in dem auch heute noch eine sehr kreative Gemeinschaft lebt, die sich in Lofts und Ateliers. Dieses Haus gehört zu einer Reihe von Einfamilienhäusern und ist eine Art Kreuzung aus städtischem Loft und Einfamilienhaus. Die offenen Wohnbereiche liegen im ersten Stockwerk. Treppen mit offenen Setzstufen verbinden diesen Bereich mit den privateren Schlafzimmern. Die offene Küche hat einen Gasofen aus Edelstahl, eine Arbeitsplatte aus Granit und Schränke aus Ahorn. Das Warmwasserheizsystem, die Boiler mit Energiesparfunktion und die elektronischen Hightech-Geräte machen diese Häuser, die perfekt gestaltet sind, ökologisch und technologisch sehr fortschrittlich. Die Vielfalt an Formen, Oberflächen und Materialien machen aus jedem Raum etwas Besonderes und unterscheiden die verschiedenen Funktionen voneinander.

This small house in San Francisco forms a cross between an urban loft and a residential home.

Cette petite habitation à San Francisco est un mélange entre un loft urbain et une habitation résidentielle.

Diese kleine Wohnung in San Francisco ist eine Mischung aus einem städtischen Loft und einem Einfamilienhaus.

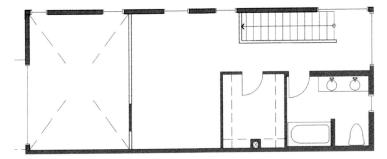

Second floor Deuxième étage Zweites Obergeschoss

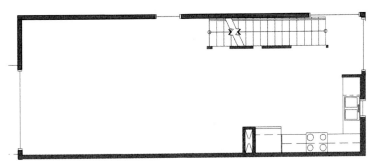

First floor Premier étage Erstes Obergeschoss

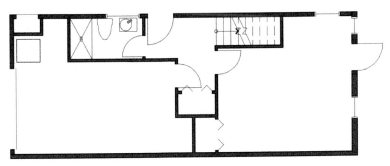

Ground floor Rez-de-chaussée Erdgeschoss

Large, open living areas span the main floor and big windows allow natural light to flow inside.

Les vastes zones de séjour ouvertes occupent l'étage principal et les grandes fenêtres permettent à la lumière naturelle d'inonder l'intérieur.

Die weiten Wohnbereiche nehmen den ersten Stock ein. Durch die großen Fenster fällt viel Tageslicht in die Räume.

House in Mosman
Maison à Mosman
Haus in Mosman

Emili Fox/Fox Johnston Architects

Closed off on three sides and only open by the rear patio, this small town house is reached by a narrow pedestrian walkway. After a lengthy process to obtain the necessary permits, the project resolved such a difficult site with the volume of two floors literally stuffed into the original building. It is a small brick block finished off with a wood facade on its only visible face and designed in a loft style, with various levels without partitions or divisions. Light is captured by large windows facing north on the ground floor and with a large open balcony with a skylight on the upper level. Another skylight casts light on the stairs and bathroom on the intermediate level. Likewise, details such as the lattice on the terrace, the translucent glass window with a texture similar to rice paper, and the parquet bring great warmth to the building.

Fermé sur trois côtés, avec une ouverture unique sur le patio arrière, l'accès à cette petite maison citadine se fait grâce à un étroit passage piétonnier. Après une longue procédure d'obtention des permis de construire nécessaires, le projet a résolu la difficulté de l'emplacement en insérant littéralement le volume de deux étages dans la structure de l'édifice original. Il en résulte un petit bloc de briques fini par une façade boisée, sur l'unique face visible, conçu dans le style loft avec différents niveaux dépourvus de cloisons et de divisions. L'orientation nord et la générosité des fenêtres permettent à la lumière d'inonder le rez-de-chaussée. Quant à l'étage supérieur, il est éclairé par le biais d'un grand balcon et d'une lucarne. Une autre lucarne assure l'éclairage de l'escalier et de la salle de bains au niveau intermédiaire. De même, des détails comme le caillebotis de la terrasse, la fenêtre de verre translucide à la texture semblable au papier de riz, ainsi que le parquet de bois imprègnent la construction de chaleur.

Dieses kleine Stadthaus ist auf drei Seiten geschlossen und öffnet sich nur zum Innenhof. Man betritt es durch einen kleinen Korridor. Nachdem man lange auf die notwendigen Baugenehmigungen warten musste, schuf man eine Lösung für den schwierigen Standort, indem man eine zweistöckige Form in die Struktur des Originalgebäudes einfügte. Es handelt sich um einen kleinen Block aus Ziegelsteinen mit einer Holzfassade auf der einzigen sichtbaren Seite, der im Stil eines Lofts mit verschiedenen Ebenen ohne Zwischenwände und Raumteiler gestaltet wurde. Die großen Fenster nach Norden lassen viel Licht in das Erdgeschoss fallen. Das gleiche geschieht im Obergeschoss durch einen offenen Balkon und ein Dachfenster. Ein anderes Dachfenster lässt Licht ins Treppenhaus und in das Bad im Zwischengeschoss fallen. Ebenso verleihen Einzelheiten wie das Geflecht der Terrasse, das Fenster mit lichtdurchlässigem Glas, das wie Reispapier aussieht, und der Parkettboden dem Gebäude Wärme.

Location plan Plan de situation Umgebungsplan

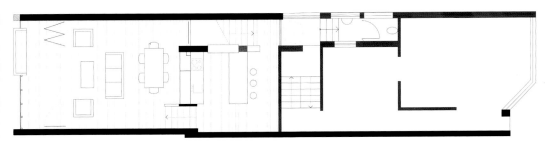

First floor Premier étage Erstes Obergeschoss

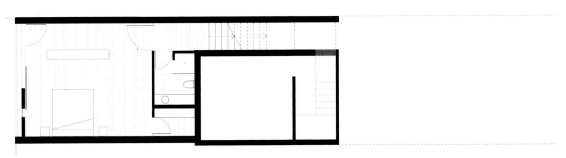

Ground floor Rez-de-chaussée Erdgeschoss

The house, surrounded by buildings, is built in the rear patio – originally a garage – of a terraced house, which is used as an office.

L'habitation, entourée d'édifices, est construite dans le patio arrière, à l'origine un garage, d'une maison individuelle employée comme bureau.

Das von Gebäuden umgebene Haus wurde im Hinterhof errichtet, der einst die Garage eines Einfamilienhauses war, das als Büro benutzt wird.

The ground floor is designed in a loft style, with various levels without partitions or divisions.

Le rez-de-chaussée est conçu dans le style loft avec différents niveaux sans cloisons ni divisions.

Das Erdgeschoss wurde im Stil eines Lofts mit verschiedenen Ebenen ohne Raumteiler gestaltet.

☐ Telegraph Hill Residence
Résidence Telegraph Hill
Residenz Telegraph Hill

House & House Architects

A small 1906 earthquake-relief home, which has accumulated additions over the decades, marks the site for this refurbished residence, located in the center of a block and surrounded by the gardens of its neighbors. Directly behind the home stands one of the largest Japanese maple trees in Northern California, and this became the focal point around which the new home evolved. Under the shadow of the city's historic Coit Tower, the house still appears to be a tiny bungalow clad with wood from the street. Inside, however, an 18-foot-high grid of windows overlooking the maple tree creates a powerful first impression. The raised first floor locates the shared rooms and opens on to a terrace garden. A curved staircase leads up to the second floor, where the more private rooms are located. Colored concrete, perforated steel and geometric fittings combine to create a unique and dynamic residence.

Une petite habitation construite pour accueillir les réfugiés du séisme de 1906, qui s'est agrandie au fil des décennies, indique l'emplacement de cette maison restaurée, située au centre d'un quartier et entourée des jardins voisins. Directement derrière l'habitation, s'élève l'un des plus grands érables japonais du nord de la Californie, devenu l'axe central autour duquel la nouvelle habitation évolue. A l'ombre de l'historique Coit Tower de la ville, la demeure apparaît depuis la rue, comme un minuscule bungalow, tout de bois revêtu. En revanche, à l'intérieur, un quadrillage de fenêtres de 5,5 m de hauteur, donnant sur l'érable, crée un impact visuel impressionnant. Le premier étage accueille les pièces communes et s'ouvre sur une terrasse avec jardin. Un escalier tout en courbes mène au deuxième étage, où se trouvent les espaces plus privés. Le béton coloré, l'acier perforé et les accessoires géométriques créent une demeure unique et dynamique.

Ein kleines Haus, das für die Menschen errichtet wurde, die 1906 vor dem Erdbeben flüchteten, wurde über die Jahrzehnte erweitert. Heute ist es ein renoviertes Wohnhaus, das im Zentrum eines Häuserblocks steht und von den Gärten der Nachbarhäuser umgeben ist. Direkt hinter dem Haus steht einer der größten japanischen Ahornbäume Nordkaliforniens. Dieser Baum ist zu dem zentralen Punkt geworden, um den herum das neue Haus entwickelt wurde. Das Haus wirkt neben dem historischen Coit Tower der Stadt wie ein winziger, mit Holz verkleideter Bungalow. Im Inneren befindet sich ein 5,5 m hohes Quadrat mit Fenstern, von dem aus man einen beeindruckenden Blick auf den Ahorn hat. Im ersten Stock befinden sich die gemeinsam genutzten Räume, die sich zu einer Terrasse mit Garten öffnen. Eine bogenförmige Treppe führt in das zweite Stockwerk, in dem sich die privaten Räume befinden. Durch den farbigen Beton, gelöcherten Stahl und die geometrischen Elemente entsteht eine einzigartige und dynamisch wirkende Wohnumgebung.

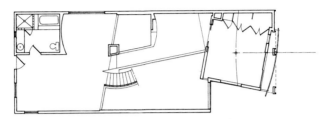

Second floor Deuxième étage Zweites Obergeschoss

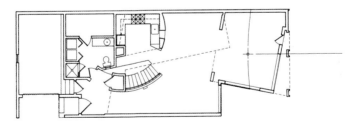

First floor Premier étage Erstes Obergeschoss

From the street, the house appears to be a tiny bungalow clad with wood.

Depuis la rue, l'habitation ressemble à un bungalow miniature revêtu de bois.

Von der Straße aus gesehen sieht das Haus wie ein winziger, mit Holz verkleideter Bungalow aus.

Colored concrete, perforated steel and geometric fittings combine to create a unique and dynamic residence.

Le béton coloré, l'acier perforé et les accessoires géométriques font de cet espace une habitation unique et dynamique.

Durch den farbigen Beton, gelöcherten Stahl und geometrische Elemente entsteht eine einzigartige und dynamisch wirkende Wohnumgebung.

☐ Randwick House
Maison Randwick
Haus Randwick

Utz-Sanby Architects

The main determinants of the extension of this typical house in the suburbs of Sydney were the proximity of the neighboring houses and the proportions of the long, narrow plot. The conversion involved the addition of a single floor containing the bedrooms which was situated adjacent to the original house. The large space left over on the ground floor was used to enlarge the living room and create a studio. The different parts of the interior are reached by a large double-height space above the dining room; this cavity also serves as an inner courtyard, creating an interior landscape that gives on to the bedrooms and providing them with openings protected from the hubbub of the city. This layout means that the exterior appearance is not too overpowering and the sunlight can fully penetrate inside, with permanent natural ventilation guaranteed in all the rooms.

L'agrandissement de cette maison typique de la banlieue de Sydney a été essentiellement déterminé par les maisons du voisinage et par les dimensions allongées du terrain. Après restructuration, la maison originale s'est vue ajouter un étage d'un niveau accueillant les chambres à coucher. Le vaste espace, resté libre au rez-de-chaussée, est utilisé pour créer une grande salle de séjour et un studio. L'accès aux différentes zones intérieures se fait par le truchement d'un grand espace sur deux hauteurs, situé au-dessus de la salle à manger. Ce grand vide sert également de patio intérieur, créant ainsi un paysage intérieur qui donne sur les chambres à coucher, ainsi dotées d'espaces ouverts protégés du tohu-bohu de la ville. De ce design ressort un aspect extérieur peu imposant qui laisse la lumière pénétrer tout l'intérieur, tout en assurant une ventilation naturelle permanente en toute saison.

Die wichtigsten Aspekte beim Ausbau dieses typischen Hauses in einem Vorort von Sydney waren die Nähe der Nachbarhäuser und das längliche, schmale Grundstück. Bei der Umgestaltung wurde dem ursprünglich Haus ein Stockwerk hinzugefügt, in dem die Schlafzimmer liegen. Der große Raum, der im Erdgeschoss leer blieb, wurde dazu benutzt, das Wohnzimmer zu erweitern und ein Atelier zu schaffen. Der Zugang zu den verschiedenen Bereichen im Inneren erfolgt durch einen großen Raum doppelter Höhe über dem Speisezimmer. Dieser Hohlraum dient auch als Innenhof, wodurch eine innere Landschaft entsteht, die auf der Seite der Schlafzimmer liegt und sie vor dem Lärm der Stadt schützt. So sieht das Haus von außen nicht allzu bedrückend aus und das Sonnenlicht dringt in alle Räume ein. Ebenso sorgt diese Struktur für die Belüftung aller Räume.

Elevations Élévations Aufrisse

Ground floor Rez-de-chaussée Erdgeschoss

First floor Premier étage Erstes Obergeschoss

The main determinants of the extension of this house were the proximity of the neighboring houses and the proportions of the long, narrow plot.

L'agrandissement de cette maison a été essentiellement déterminé par les maisons du voisinage et par les dimensions allongées du terrain.

Die wichtigsten Aspekte beim Ausbau dieses typischen Hauses in Sydney waren die Nähe der Nachbarhäuser und das längliche, schmale Grundstück.

The large space left over on the ground floor was used to enlarge the living room and create a studio.

Le vaste espace, resté libre au rez-de-chaussée, permet de créer une grande salle de séjour et un studio.

Der große Raum, der im Erdgeschoss leer blieb, wurde dazu benutzt, das Wohnzimmer zu erweitern und ein Atelier zu schaffen.

PML House
Maison PML
Haus PML

Manuel Cerdá Pérez, Julio Vila Liante

Located in Albuixech, this small house offers an alternative to the typical suburban house model. The building's structure is characterized by three longitudinal lines that demarcate the space: two party walls and one wall completely divide the house. The widest space is destined for the bedroom areas and the narrowest for circulation and services. A minimalist staircase that starts at the entrance level rises perpendicularly along the street facade. All the floors have transparent, open spaces, while the upper level can be subdivided by sliding birch wood walls. The climax to the spatial flow is provided by the covered rooftop terrace, with its views of the surrounding orchards and the Mediterranean.

Située à Albuixech, cette maison de taille modeste est une alternative au modèle type d'habitat suburbain. La structure de l'édifice présente trois lignes longitudinales qui délimitent l'espace : deux transversales et un mur divisent entièrement la demeure. L'espace le plus large est consacré à la zone des chambres à coucher et le plus étroit aux zones de circulation et de services. Un escalier au design minimaliste, partant du niveau de l'entrée, grimpe perpendiculairement le long de la façade de la rue. Tous les étages sont dotés d'espaces ouverts et diaphanes, le niveau supérieur pouvant être subdivisé grâce à des cloisons coulissantes en bois de bouleau. A l'apogée de cette fluctuation de l'espace, l'accès à la terrasse couverte permet de jouir des vues sur les vergers environnants et sur la Méditerranée.

Dieses kleine Haus in einem Vorort von Valencia, Albuixech, bietet eine Alternative zu den sonst typischen Häusern in den Außenbezirken. An der Struktur des Gebäudes befinden sich drei Längslinien, die den Raum aufteilen; zwei Zwischenwände und eine weitere Wand. Im größten Bereich liegen die Schlafzimmer und im kleinsten die funktionellen Räume und Durchgangsräume. Eine minimalistisch gestaltete Treppe, die am Eingang beginnt, steigt senkrecht an der Fassade zur Straße entlang nach oben. Alle Wohnungen sind offen und fast transparent. Die obere Ebene kann durch Schiebepaneele aus Birkenholz unterteilt werden. Der Zugang zur überdachten Dachterrasse bildet eine Art Höhepunkt in diesem Raum: von hier aus hat man einen Blick auf die umliegenden Gärten und das Mittelmeer.

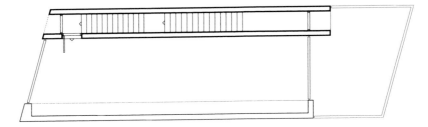

Roof plan Plan du toit Dachgeschoss

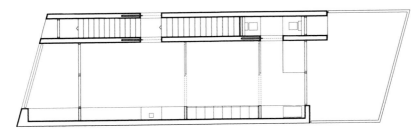

First floor Premier étage Erstes Obergeschoss

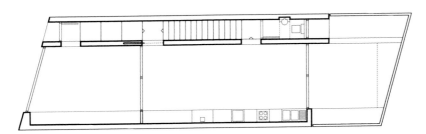

Ground floor Rez-de-chaussée Erdgeschoss

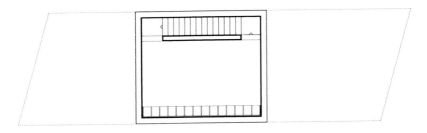

Basement Sous-sol Kellergeschoss

The building's structure is characterized by three longitudinal lines that demarcate the space.

La structure de l'édifice présente trois lignes longitudinales délimitant l'espace.

An der Struktur des Gebäudes befinden sich drei Längslinien, die den Raum aufteilen.

A minimalist staircase that starts at the entrance level rises perpendicularly along the street façade.

Un escalier au design minimaliste, partant de l'entrée, grimpe perpendiculairement le long de la façade.

Eine minimalistisch gestaltete Treppe, die am Eingang beginnt, steigt senkrecht an der Fassade zur Straße entlang nach oben.

House in Motoazabu
Maison à Motoazabu
Haus in Motoazabu

Mutsue Hayakusa, Cell Space Architects

This house consists of three floors of reduced dimensions connected by a spiral stairway. The home has an unusual shape due to the lack of space available for erecting the building. To overcome this inconvenience the architects decided to make use of angles and contrasting elements. A curved glass surface separates the entrance area from the garage. The curvature of the glass helps minimize the constrained feeling of the space. The private quarters of the house are flooded with the natural light that filters through the garage, which is completely white. One of the main objectives of the architects was to emphasize the connection between urban and rural life, visually and physically, so the car, an urban utility, becomes an integral part of the residence. At night, the reflections on the windows seemingly make the house expand horizontally and make it appear more spacious.

Cette maison est structurée sur trois étages reliés par un esca-lier en spirale ancré sur un étage aux dimensions réduites. L'ha-bitation revêt une forme inhabituelle, due au manque d'espace pour construire l'édifice. Cet inconvénient a été surmonté en optant pour une alternance d'angles et de contrastes. Une superficie en verre tout en courbes divise la zone d'entrée du garage. Cette linéarité particulière du verre permet d'amplifier la perception globale de cet espace si restreint. La lumière naturelle inonde le garage, entièrement blanc, qu'elle traverse pour atteindre l'espace privé de l'habitation. Les architectes ont proposé, entre autres, d'accentuer le lien, tant visuel que phy-sique, entre la vie urbaine et rurale, où la voiture, outil utilitaire de la ville, intègre la résidence. La nuit, les reflets sur le verre des fenêtres offrent une vision horizontale et accroissent la sensation d'espace.

Dieses Haus besteht aus drei Stockwerken, die über eine Wen-deltreppe miteinander verbunden sind, und es steht auf einem relativ kleinen Grundstück. Das Haus hat aufgrund des knapp bemessenen Platzes eine sehr ungewöhnliche Form. Um diesen Platzmangel auszugleichen, benutzte man verschiedene Winkel und Kontraste. Ein gekrümmte verglaste Fläche trennt den Ein-fahrtsbereich zur Garage ab. Die besondere Linearität des Glases ermöglicht es, diesen kleinen Raum größer wirken zu lassen. Das Tageslicht dringt in die Garage ein und gelangt in den privaten Bereich des Hauses. Die Architekten wollten sowohl visuell als auch physisch die Verbindung zwischen dem städtischen und ländlichen Leben verstärken, in dem das Auto, ein Werkzeug der Stadt, zu einem Teil der Wohnung wird. Nachts glaubt man, aufgrund der Reflexe auf dem Glas der Fen-ster eine Art Horizont zu sehen, und der Eindruck von Weite wird noch verstärkt.

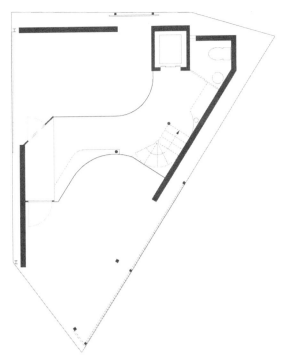

Plan Plan Grundriss

Elevation Élévation Aufriss

This small home has an unusual shape, due to the lack of space available for erecting the building.

Cette habitation de petite taille revêt une forme inhabituelle, due au manque d'espace disponible pour l'édification de l'immeuble.

Diese kleine Wohnung hat eine sehr ungewöhnliche Form. Dies ist auf den relativ knapp bemessenen Raum bei der Errichtung des Gebäudes zurückzuführen.

A spiral staircase connects the building's three floors, while the skylight in the ceiling allows natural light to flow into each of the rooms.

Un escalier en spirale relie les trois étages de l'édifice et la lucarne de toit permet à la lumière naturelle de pénétrer l'ensemble de l'espace.

Eine Wendeltreppe verbindet die drei Etagen des Gebäudes und durch das Dachfenster fällt viel Tageslicht in alle Räume.

☐ Dwelling in A Coruña
Habitation à A Coruña
Wohnung in A Coruña

Toni García

This house/studio goes against the norm that discourages the construction of living spaces on the ground floor. To prove that it is possible to create a place to live with the limited means of most young people, some have turned to refurbishing spaces like this, one of the many silent and abandoned street level spaces among the traffic-filled streets of an autistic city that has turned its back on nature. The entire small building can be defined as a large piece of furniture that contains everything that is needed in the house and fills the limited space with light and air. Each architectural feature defines a multifunctional vital organ. The various elements inside transform themselves into a mailbox, umbrella stand, filing cabinet, work table, and dressing room, while the entrance door becomes a dresser. Santiago Caneda painted an elegy to nature in the middle of the front wall, and an indoor garden grows around the bathtub.

Cette maison/bureau s'oppose à la règle qui interdit de construire des logements sur les bas-fonds. Pour créer un lieu de vie correspondant aux moyens financiers limités des jeunes, on a aménagé les terrains vagues abandonnés entre les rues trépidantes de circulation dans une ville autiste qui s'éloigne de la nature. Le volume réduit s'assimile à un énorme meuble qui case dans des coins les ustensiles domestiques nécessaires et qui illumine et ventile cet espace limité. Chaque organisation architecturale définit un organe vital aux fonctions multiples. A l'intérieur, les différents éléments se transforment en boîte aux lettre, porte-parapluie, classeur, plan de travail et dressing, et la porte d'entrée se transforme en meuble portemanteau. Le tableau mural de la façade, peint par Santiago Caneda, et le jardin intérieur qui pousse autour de la baignoire font l'éloge de la nature.

Diese kleine Wohnung lehnt sich gegen die Vorschriften auf, die die Errichtung von Wohnungen im Erdgeschoss verhindern wollen. Um eine Umgebung zu schaffen, in der man trotz der begrenzten ökonomischen Möglichkeiten komfortabel wohnen kann, entschloss man sich zum Umbau eines der vielen Erdgeschosse, die in den verkehrsreichen Straßen einer sich immer mehr von der Natur entfernenden Stadt leer stehen. Die kleine Wohnung gleicht einem riesigen Möbelstück, in dem die notwendigen Elemente eines Hauses untergebracht sind und das für Licht und Belüftung in dem kleinen Raum sorgt. Jeder Bereich bestimmt ein multifunktionelles, lebensnotwendiges Organ. Die verschiedenen Elemente im Inneren werden zu einem Briefkasten, einem Schirmständer, einem Aktenschrank, einem Arbeitstisch und einem Ankleideraum, und die Eingangstür wird zu einem Ankleideraum. Das Mauerbild von Santiago Caneda an der Fassade und der innere Garten, der um eine Badewanne entstanden ist, sind ein Loblied auf die Natur.

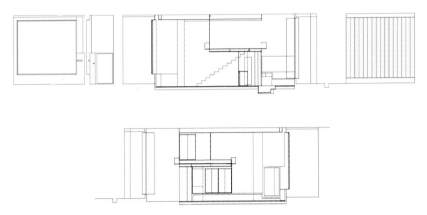

Sections Sections Schnitte

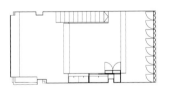

Plans Plans Grundrisse

The entire small building can be defined as a large piece of furniture that contains everything that is needed in the house and fills the limited space with light and air.

L'ensemble du petit édifice peut se définir comme une grande pièce de mobilier contenant tout ce qui est nécessaire à l'habitation et remplissant l'espace réduit de lumière et d'air.

Dieses kleine Gebäude kann man insgesamt als ein großes Möbelelement definieren, das alles Notwendige für die Wohnung enthält und den begrenzten Raum mit Licht und Luft füllt.

⌂ Each architectural feature defines a multifunctional vital organ. The various elements inside transform themselves according to need.

Chaque élément architectural détermine un organe vital multifonctionnel. Les divers éléments intérieurs se transforment au gré des nécessités.

Jeder Bereich bestimmt ein multifunktionelles, lebendiges Organ. Die verschiedenen Elemente im Inneren werden den Anforderungen der Bewohner entsprechend verändert.

The kitchen is very small but fully equipped with the latest technology.

La cuisine, aux dimensions très réduites, est entièrement dotée d'un équipement à la pointe de la technologie.

Die Küche ist sehr klein, aber vollständig mit der neuesten Technologie ausgestattet.

☐ Floating Platform
Plateforme flottante
Schwebende Plattform

N55

Enclosing a space large enough to house four people, this light and inexpensive geometric shape is very flexible and easy to assemble. This solution to a simple puzzle was dictated by the requirements of its users, who were able to freely mold the four-sided volume with a surface area of less than 215 sq. ft. A floating platform, made of interlocking stainless steel modules that can be assembled by hand, accentuates the lightness and volatile nature of this shell designed to enhance a tranquil lifestyle. The house, as well as the platform on which it stands, are made with materials that are exceptionally lightweight. The complexity of its exterior conceals a structure put together by hand, that can be assembled and dismounted as often as needed and transported from place to place without difficulty.

Cette forme géométrique très polyvalente au montage très facil configure un habitacle économique aux dimensions permettant d'accueillir quatre personnes. La solution à ce simple casse-tête dépend des besoins des usagers qui peuvent façonner à leur gré ce volume tétraèdre d'une surface de 20 m². Une plateforme flottante – composée de modules entrelacés d'acier inoxydable que l'on peut monter manuellement – accentue la légèreté et la volatilité de cette armature pensée pour profiter d'un style de vie paisible. L'habitation elle-même et la plateforme qui la soutient sont construites avec matériaux très légers. La complexité de son apparence masque une construction qui se réalise manuellement, pouvant être montée et démontée à volonté et déplacée sans trop d'efforts.

Diese leichte und billige, vielseitige und einfach zu montierende und zu benutzende geometrische Figur formt einen Wohnraum für vier Personen. Dieses einfache Puzzlekonzept wurde durch die Ansprüche der Benutzer geprägt, die diesen Raum nun in Form eines Tetraeders mit 20 m² Fläche frei gestalten können. Eine schwebende Plattform, die von miteinander verflochtenen Modulen aus Edelstahl gebildet und manuell montiert wird, unterstreicht die Leichtigkeit und Flüchtigkeit dieses Gerüstes, das dazu bestimmt ist, das Wohnen angenehm zu machen. Sowohl die Wohnung an sich als auch die Plattform, die sie hält, wurden mit so wenig Material wie möglich konstruiert, so dass sie sehr leicht wirken. Das komplexe Erscheinungsbild verbirgt eine Konstruktion, die von Hand errichtet wird und die man so oft man es wünscht montieren und demontieren kann, um sie ohne große Anstrengungen von einem Ort zum anderen zu transportieren.

This support, made of triangular modules, can be folded like a sheet of paper to create a three-dimensional structure.

Ce support, constitué de modules triangulaires, se plie comme une feuille de papier pour créer une structure tridimensionnelle.

Diese Befestigung aus dreieckigen Modulen kann wie ein Stück Papier gefaltet werden, um eine dreidimensionale Struktur zu schaffen.

Pixel House
Maison Pixel
Pixel Haus

Faulkner & Chapman Landscape Design

The Pixel house was designed with a repeating pattern that is reminiscent of the pixels in digital images. The owners were interested in a design that would allow them to share part of the exterior with the other people in the neighborhood. The house is built on a trapezoidal floor plan and makes use of a large variety of materials to create an unusual building. The design was made by using sequences of angled bricks that resemble pixels. The bricks also provide a very tangible sense of both the scale and the building process. A semi-private area was created at the back of the house; this is directly accessible from the front part of the residence. In fact, all the neighbors are free to come into this space; one of the owner's requirements was to be able to use this setting as a community center during the day and as a private area at night and at weekends.

La maison Pixel a été conçue à partir d'une structure récurrente qui rappelle les pixels des images digitales. Les propriétaires voulaient un projet permettant de partager l'extérieur avec les autres voisins du quartier. La maison se développe sur un plan orthogonal en déclinant une grande variété de matériaux qui lui confère une structure originale. Le design se base sur la disposition orthogonale d'une succession de briques, imitant les pixels. Les briques contribuent également à ce que l'échelle et le processus de construction soient perçus de façon tangible. La zone arrière de la maison accueille un espace semi-privé auquel il est possible d'accéder directement depuis l'avant de l'habitation. De fait, n'importe quel voisin est invité à pénétrer ces espaces. Une des exigences des propriétaires est de pouvoir utiliser cet espace comme centre communautaire durant le jour et comme zone privée durant la nuit et les week-ends.

Das Pixel Haus wurde mit einer sich wiederholenden Struktur gestaltet, die an die Pixel digitalisierter Bilder erinnert. Die Eigentümer wünschten sich ein Haus, in dem sie einen Teil der Außenanlagen gemeinsam mit den Nachbarn im Viertel benutzen konnten. Das Haus hat einen rechtwinkligen Grundriss und es wurden viele verschiedene Materialien eingesetzt, so dass eine interessante Struktur entstand. Bei der Gestaltung ging man von dem vorhandenen Rechteck aus und verwendete Sequenzen von Ziegelsteinen, die Pixel imitieren. Die Ziegel trugen auch dazu bei, den Maßstab und den Bauprozess greifbarer zu machen. Im hinteren Teil des Hauses schuf man einen halbprivaten Bereich, den man direkt vom vorderen Teil aus betritt. Tatsächlich sind auch alle Nachbarn in diesem Bereich willkommen. Die Kunden hatten sich gewünscht, dass dieser Bereich zu einem gemeinsamen Zentrum für den Tag und einem privaten Raum in den Nächten und an den Wochenenden wird.

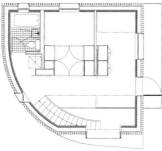

Plans Plans Grundrisse

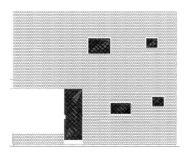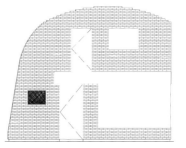

Elevations Élévations Aufrisse

The tiered sequence of the bricks is barely noticeable inside the structure, which is concave and completely smooth.

L'échelonnement des briques est à peine visible au sein de la structure concave et entièrement uniforme.

Die stufenförmige Sequenz der Ziegelsteine ist im Inneren der Struktur kaum zu bemerken, sie ist konkav und völlig einheitlich.

A semi-private area was created at the back of the house; this is directly accessible from the front part of the residence.

L'arrière de l'habitation contient une zone semi-privée à laquelle on accède directement depuis l'avant de la résidence.

Es wurde ein halb privater Bereich im hinteren Teil des Hauses geschaffen, zu dem man direkt vom vorderen Teil des Gebäudes aus gelangt.

☐ Triangular House
Maison triangulaire
Dreieckiges Haus

Masaki Endoh

The majority of buildings in Japan are becoming increasingly smaller as a result of the ever-expanding metropolis. This situation demands well-lit and ventilated rooms to create a feeling of comfort and spaciousness. This residence, spanning less than 1,000 sq. ft, was designed with a triangular structure, which enabled the architects to capture the maximum amount of sunlight inside the house without surpassing the legal height limits. It consists of a steel panel with polyester insulation attached to a horizontal wall, which was designed to shine brightly and creates an unusual pentagram structure. A translucent Goretex membrane was inserted between the panel and the glass; this highly efficient material, which protects against ultraviolet rays, is often used in winter clothing.

Au Japon, la majorité des édifices sont de plus en plus contraints de réduire leur taille face à l'expansion croissante de la métropole. Dans les emplacements de ce type, il est essentiel que les constructions disposent d'espaces lumineux et bien ventilés pour accroître la sensation d'espace et de confort. Dotée d'une surface inférieure à 85 m², l'habitation est conçue comme une structure triangulaire afin d'obtenir un éclairage naturel maximum à l'intérieur sans dépasser les limites de hauteur légales. Cette structure est composée d'un treillis d'acier avec une isolation en polyester montée sur le mur longitudinal, conçue pour briller intensément et crée une structure originale rappelant une portée. Entre ce treillis et le verre, il y a une membrane translucide en goretex, matière protégeant des rayons ultraviolets, souvent utilisée dans les vêtements d'hiver.

In Japan werden aufgrund des großen städtischen Wachstums die Gebäude immer kleiner. Besonders wichtig ist es an solchen Standorten, dass es in den Gebäuden Räume mit viel Luft und Licht gibt, so dass der Eindruck von Weite und Komfort entsteht. Diese unter 85 m² große Wohnung wurde als eine dreieckige Struktur angelegt, um so viel Tageslicht wie möglich hinein zu lassen und auch die gesetzlichen Vorschriften hinsichtlich der Gebäudehöhe nicht zu überschreiten. Die Struktur von Natural Wedge besteht aus einem Flechtwerk aus Stahl, das mit Polyester isoliert und auf eine Längswand montiert ist und intensiv glänzt. Dieses Isolationsmaterial lässt eine originale Struktur entstehen, die wie Notenlinien aussieht. Zwischen dem Flechtwerk und dem Glas befindet sich eine lichtdurchlässige Membran aus Goretex, ein Material, das vor UV-Licht schützt und oft für Winterkleidung benutzt wird.

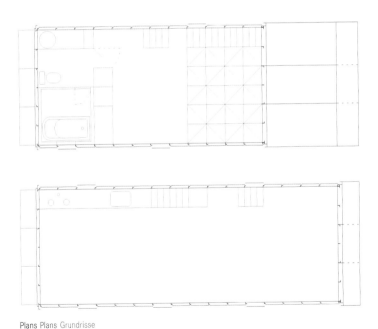

Plans Plans Grundrisse

The crystalline structure becomes a magical object when light flows in, making the space come alive.

La structure à l'aspect cristallin se métamorphose en objet magique lorsque la lumière y pénètre, donnant vie à l'espace.

Die gläsern wirkende Struktur wird zu einem magischen Objekt, wenn das Licht eindringt. Der Raum wird plötzlich lebendig.

The interior is open and uninterrupted, integrating the different floors connected by a metal staircase.

L'intérieur est ouvert et continu, intégrant les divers niveaux reliés par un escalier métallique.

Das Innere ist offen und ununterbrochen und integriert die verschiedenen Stockwerke, die über eine Treppe aus Metall verbunden sind.

Photo credits Crédits photographiques Fotonachweis